DEMETRIOS I. FALLIS
EVRYTANIA

DEMETRIOS I. FALLIS

EVRYTANIA

ANCIENT HISTORY AND LEGEND

Translation and Introduction by
George C. Papademetriou

SOMERSET HALL PRESS
Boston, Massachusetts

© Copyright 2023 Demetrios Ioannis Fallis
(all rights reserved throughout the world)
English Translation by George C. Papademetriou

Published by Somerset Hall Press
416 Commonwealth Avenue, Suite 612
Boston, Massachusetts 02215
www.somersethallpress.com

Cover image of King Evrytos was inspired by Demetrios Fallis and drawn by Panagiotis Liaskou.

ISBN: 978-1-935-244-27-1
E-Book: 978-1-935-244-28-8

LIBRARY OF CONGRESS CATALOGING-IN-PUBLICATION DATA

Names: Fallis, Demetrios Ioannis, author. | Papademetriou, George C., translator, writer of introduction.
Title: Evrytania : ancient history and legend / by Demetrios Ioannis Fallis; translation and introduction by George C. Papademetriou.
Other titles: Evrytania. English
Description: Boston, Massachusetts : Somerset Hall Press, [2022] | "English translation." | Includes bibliographical references and index. | Summary: "A history of ancient Evrytania, a region of Greece, with a discussion of the legends and archeological findings"-- Provided by publisher.
Identifiers: LCCN 2022053252 (print) | LCCN 2022053253 (ebook) | ISBN 9781935244271 (paperback) | ISBN 9781935244288 (ebook)
Subjects: LCSH: Eurytania (Greece)--History. | Eurytania (Greece)--Antiquities. | Legends--Greece--Eurytania. | Excavations (Archaeology)--Greece--Eurytania.
Classification: LCC DF261.E96 F3513 2022 (print) | LCC DF261. E96 (ebook) | DDC 938/.3--dc23/eng/20221109

LC record available at https://lccn.loc.gov/2022053252
LC ebook record available at https://lccn.loc.gov/2022053253

CONTENTS

Acknowledgments   7
Foreword (in English and Greek),
    by Mayor Kostas Bakoyannis   9
Maps of Greece and Evrytania   16

Introduction,
    by Rev. George C. Papademetriou   19

I. Evrytania
    A Place with a Very Ancient History   25
    Buried Historical Treasure   27
    Protachaioi, the First People who lived in Evrytania   30
    The Earliest People in Evrytania   32
    The Language   33
    Religious Life in Ancient Evrytania   36
    The Boundaries of Ancient Evrytania   39
    The Expansion of the Boundaries of Ancient Evrytania   40

II. Evrytos—History—Legend (Thryllos)
    The Originator of the Evrytanians   43
    Mythology   44
    Tradition   46
    The Origin of Evrytos   47
    Oechalia   50
    The First Oechalia   51
    Oechalia at Klapsi   52
    The Oracle of Odysseus   54
    Precise Location of the Oracle of Odysseus   56
    The Aetolian Commonwealth   57
    Unification of the Aetolians in 322 BC   59
    From the Mythical Times   61

III. Callium

In the Wrong Place	65
The Contemporary History of the Seat of Callium	67
Mistaken Acceptance of Soteriades's Position	71
Callium, the Capital City	74
Position of Some Historians	75
The Local Tradition Regarding Callium	77
Findings of Ancient Objects at Klapsi	79
Agios Leonides	80
Historical Proof	85
Thucydides	86
Pausanias	87

IV. Kokkalia

Forgotten Evrytanian Glory	93
The Invasion of the Galatians	95
The Greeks Completely Lost their Confidence	101
The Struggle that Lies Ahead	105
The Barbarians were Alarmed	110
On their Mothers' Breasts	113
From the Same Path	116
Strategic Position	120
No Ambivalence	122
Research *In Loco*	123
How Kokkalia Was Named Before	127
Kallidromo	129
They were Full of Wrath against the Galatians	132
Monument to the Immortal Glory of the Aetolians	135

Endnotes	139
Afterword, by Nicholas and Jane Kourtis	155
Pictures of Evrytania	157
About the Author	165
About the Translator	167

ACKNOWLEDGMENTS

We gratefully acknowledge the generous support of the Evrytanian Association of America "Velouchi" and the Panevrytanikis Enosis of Greece for the publication of this translation. The visionary leaders of these organizations appreciate the importance of the ancient history of Evrytania and understand the need to spread the message of this history to new generations and in the United States and other parts of the world.

TRANSLATOR'S
ACKNOWLEDGMENTS

First, I would like to acknowledge and thank Demetrios Fallis, the author of the original Greek version of this book. Through the years, we have had many interesting conversations about Evrytania and ancient history.

Furthermore, I would like to thank Mayor Kostas Bakoyannis, the mayor of Athens and formerly of Karpenisi, Greece, for providing such an insightful Foreword. I have known him and his family, including his mother Dora Bakoyannis, a dedicated public official, for many years. He has been an innovative and creative mayor who has worked tirelessly to improve Athens and Karpenisi for the betterment of the residents of today and the future. He also appreciates the importance of understanding the past. In addition, thank you to Eliza Konstantinidi, who efficiently and graciously coordinated our correspondence with the Mayor's office.

My gratitude to Professor Vasilios Tsigkos who provided valuable information about Evrytania and assisted me and Mr. Fallis in many ways.

Last but not least, I would like to thank Jane P. Kourtis, Nicholas F. Kourtis, Susan Metropol, Dean Papademetriou, and Deacon Pavlos Soterelis for their assistance in typing, editing, and publishing this book.

With help from God and the assistance of these people, as well as others who have assisted me in other projects, I am happy to have this English translation published.

FOREWORD

Kostas Bakoyannis
Mayor of Athens,
Former Governor of Central Greece,
and Former Mayor of Karpenisi, Greece

It is a special honor for me to write this Foreword for the book *Evrytania: Ancient History and Legend* by Mr. Demetrios Fallis, with an expert translation and additional notes by Rev. Fr. George Papademetriou, thus giving our expatriates and others the opportunity to read and learn the rich history of motherland Evrytania.

Two remarkable Evrytanians, who love their native land, set out to shed light on the ancient history of their place, starting from ancient times. Mr. Fallis's book is the result of years of research and study. His zeal and his love for Evrytania led him on this exciting journey in time and history. This was followed by the initiative of Rev. Fr. Papademetriou to proceed with the translation into English of Mr. Fallis's original research, so that those in the diaspora can more deeply appreciate the historical depth of Evrytania.

Evrytania is not only its high and untracked mountains, its picturesque villages, and its beauties of nature, blessed by God. It is not only the glorious history of the heroes who fought and were sacrificed during the Turkish occupation and the World Wars, nor the dark days of the civil war, which brought gloom throughout the land. Evrytania is also the land born from its first King Evrytos, with a history beginning much earlier than 3000 BC.

Thus, within the pages of the book you hold in your hands, the author and the translator want to let the reader learn about the birth of Evrytania, the myths and legends surrounding it, the long-lived traditions, as well as the great history revealed by the archaeological findings so far. Ancient Kallion, Kokallia, Oichalia, Evrytos, Hercules, the heroic women of Aetolia, and all the history and culture of ancient Evrytania will travel to the other side of the world.

Our brothers and sisters, the expatriate Evrytanians of America, including the third and fourth generations, as well as others who love Evrytania or want to learn about it, will now have the pleasure to read about the fascinating history of Evrytania in the English language. Through the legends and illustrative images described by the author's painstaking pen, and as carefully translated and enriched by the translator, you will travel back in time, learning everything about the beginning of our generation.

Foreword

This book should be part of the library of all Evrytanians, but also of the library of everyone who loves and respects history, and especially Greek history. We owe a huge thank you to the historian and researcher Mr. Dimitris Fallis for his very important work, which is undoubtedly a great legacy for all future generations, as well as to the respected Rev. Fr. George Papademetriou, who contributed to the publication of the book in English.

As an Evrytanian myself, I am grateful to you. Enjoy the book!

ΠΡΟΛΟΓΟΣ

Κώστας Μπακογιάννης
Δήμαρχος Αθήνας και Πρόειν Δήμαρχος Καρπενισίου

Αποτελεί ιδιαίτερη τιμή για εμένα να προλογίσω το βιβλίο «Ευρυτανία: Αρχαία Ιστορία και Θρύλος» του κ. Δημητρίου Φαλλή, την μετάφραση του οποίου επιμελήθηκε εξαιρετικά ο πατήρ Γεώργιος Παπαδημητρίου, δίνοντας έτσι στους ομογενείς μας τη δυνατότητα να διαβάσουν και να μάθουν την πλούσια ιστορία της Μητέρας Ευρυτανίας.

Δύο αξιόλογοι Ευρυτάνες, που αγαπούν την γενέθλια γη τους, θέλησαν να ρίξουν φως στην αρχαία ιστορία του τόπου τους, η οποία ξεκινά από αρχαιοτάτων χρόνων.

Το βιβλίο του κ. Φαλλή είναι αποτέλεσμα χρόνιας έρευνας και μελέτης. Ο ζήλος του και η αγάπη του για την Ευρυτανία, τον οδήγησε σε αυτό το συναρπαστικό ταξίδι στο χρόνο και στην ιστορία.

Η Ευρυτανία δεν είναι μόνο τα ψηλά και απάτητα βουνά της, τα γραφικά χωριά της και οι ομορφιές της φύσης, με τις οποίες την ευλόγησε ο Θεός. Δεν είναι μόνο η ένδοξη ιστορία των ηρώων που αγωνίστηκαν και θυσιάστηκαν επί Τουρκοκρατίας και κατά τη διάρκεια των Παγκοσμίων Πολέμων, ούτε οι μαύρες μέρες του εμφυλίου πολέμου, που την σκοτείνιασαν απ' άκρη σε άκρη. Η Ευρυτανία είναι η γη που γεννήθηκε από τον πρώτο της βασιλιά Εύρυτο, με την ιστορία της να ξεκινά πολύ πιο πριν από το 3000 π.Χ.

Μέσα, λοιπόν, από τις σελίδες του βιβλίου που κρατάτε στα χέρια σας, ο συγγραφέας θέλει να κάνει γνωστό στον αναγνώστη τη γέννηση της Ευρυτανίας, τους μύθους και τους θρύλους γύρω από αυτή, τις μακρόβιες παραδόσεις, αλλά και την σπουδαία ιστορία που αποδεικνύεται από τα έως τώρα αρχαιολογικά ευρήματα.

Το Αρχαίο Κάλλιον, τα Κοκάλλια, η Οιχαλία, ο Εύρυτος, ο Ηρακλής, οι ηρωικές γυναίκες της Αιτωλίας και όλη η ιστορία και η κουλτούρα της αρχαίας Ευρυτανίας θα ταξιδέψουν στην άλλη άκρη της γης, μετά την πρωτοβουλία του πατρός Γεωργίου Παπαδημητρίου, να προχωρήσει στη μετάφραση της αρχικής έρευνας του κ. Φαλλή.

Τα αδέρφια μας, οι ομογενείς Ευρυτάνες της Αμερικής, τρίτης και τέταρτης γενιάς, θα έχουν πλέον τη χαρά να διαβάσουν τη συναρπαστική ιστορία της Ευρυτανίας στην καθομολογουμένη τους. Μέσα από τους θρύλους και τις παραστατικές εικόνες που περιγράφο-

Introduction 15

νται από τη δεινή πένα του συγγραφέα, θα ταξιδέψουν μαζί του πίσω στο χρόνο, μαθαίνοντας τα πάντα για την αρχή της γενέτειράς μας.

Το παρόν βιβλίο πρέπει να βρίσκεται στη βιβλιοθήκη κάθε Ευρυτάνα, αλλά και στη βιβλιοθήκη κάθε Έλληνα που αγαπά και σέβεται την ιστορία. Οφείλουμε ένα τεράστιο ευχαριστώ στον ιστοριοδίφη και ερευνητή κ. Δημήτρη Φαλλήγια το τόσο σημαντικό του έργο, το οποίο αποτελεί αναμφισβήτητα σπουδαία παρακαταθήκη για όλες τις επόμενες γενιές, καθώς και στο σεβαστό πατέρα Γεώργιο, που χωρίς τη δική του συμβολή δεν θα υπήρχε η έκδοση του βιβλίου «Ευρυτανία: Αρχαία Ιστορία και Θρύλος» στην αγγλική γλώσσα.

Ως Ευρυτάνας σας είμαι ευγνώμων. Καλή ανάγνωση!

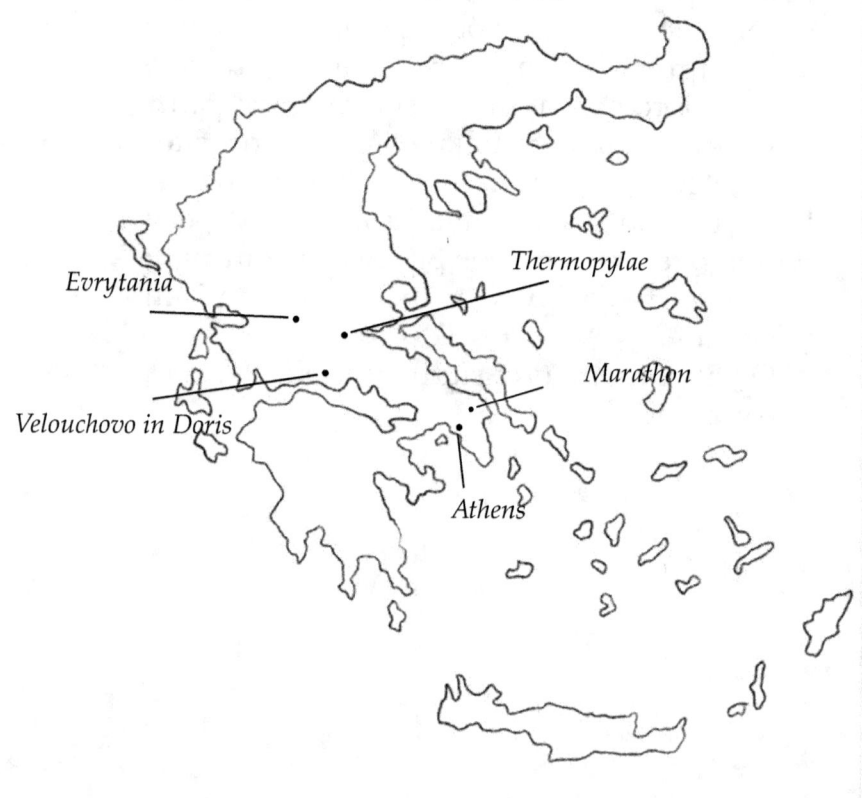

GREECE

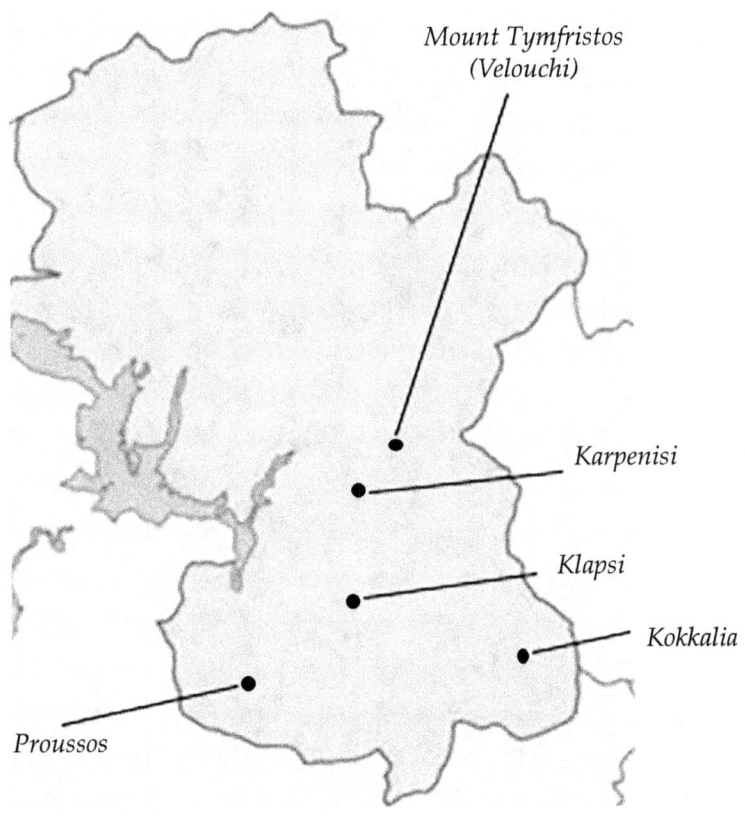

INTRODUCTION

George C. Papademetriou

The mountainous land of Evrytania, a province in central Greece, has an illustrious history. Evrytanians and their descendants in Greece, the United States, and around the world are justifiably proud of this history.

In Ottoman times, the Greeks in Evrytania resisted the Ottomans as much as they could and preserved their culture and language. Two Evrytanians stand out during this period. In the seventeenth century, Evgenios Yiannoules the Aitolos opened a famous school called the Hellenic Museum of Agrafa. His brilliant student, the Venerable Anastasios Gordios, went on to study in Padua, Italy, and came back to Evrytania as a teacher and a doctor.

During the Greek Revolution of 1821, the soldiers known as *armatoloi* were instrumental in the success of the Revolution. They were Greeks, many of them from Evrytania, who had been trained in bearing arms by the Ottomans to keep order. During the Revolution, they used their training by the Ottomans to fight for and with their fellow Greeks. Evrytania was one of the first parts of Greece that was liberated at the same time as Peloponnesos because of the bravery of these Evrytanian warriors.

During World War II, there were many examples of bravery by Evrytanians. A general originally from the village of Braha in Evrytania led his troops in Epiros to fight the Italian army despite orders from his superiors in Athens to retreat. They pushed back the Italian army. After the war, a statue of him was erected in Ioannina for saving the people there.

The villagers of Proussos resisted the German Army in order to protect the miracle-working icon of the Virgin Mary. The Nazis were going to burn down the monastery in Proussos in retaliation against the Greek resistance. The villagers intervened to save the icon, known as Panagia Proussiotissa. The story and a picture of the icon are included in the book *The Virgin Mary in Holy Icons and Stories* (Somerset Hall Press, 2021).

Although the history of Evrytania is so illustrious, many people, including Evrytanians and their descendants, are unaware that this history is in fact much more ancient. The author, Mr. Demetrios Fallis, and the translator, Fr. George Papademetriou, who both hail from Evrytania, wish to educate the reader about this ancient history.

There was a great and developed culture in ancient Evrytania, also known as Aetolia, of which we must be proud. "The Aetolians—mentioned for the first time in an inscription on an Athenian stele from the year 367/366 BC—relying on a treaty with Akarnanians, expanded their power in Central Greece." (Herman Bengtson, *History of Greece, From the Beginnings to the Byzantine Era*, Trans. and updated by Edmund F. Bluedow: University of Ottawa Press (1988), p. 299). The historian Thucydides says, "The Aetolian nation was great and with great warriors."

Yet people have inhabited the region of Evrytania for even longer—at least 5,000 years. Because of the rugged terrain, the Evrytanian people have been self-sufficient but have also shown great bravery when outsiders have tried to invade their land. As the author Demetrios Fallis states in the book, "The Evrytanians stood strong in the passing of thousands of years with their local customs, with their strange and rough uncompromised character..."

The present book begins with a chapter on these first Evrytanians and the Evrytanian region. The next chapter focuses on Evrytos, the founder of Evrytania, including facts and legends about him. As described in these chapters, there was a great and developed culture in ancient Evrytania or Aetolia. This is witnessed especially by the classical historians Pausanias and Thucydides, who wrote about the ancient Commonwealth of Aetolia, which included Evrytania. A fifth century AD Christian church edifice dedicated to Agios (Saint) Leonides also provides evidence of an older civilization.

The next chapter addresses the ancient city of Callium and argues that it was located in Evrytania and specifically in present-day Klapsi. This is important because of the destruction that occurred in Callium. The people of Klapsi still have memories of Callium that have passed down through the generations.

The final chapter expounds on the dramatic events related to the invasion of mainland Greece by the Galatians in 279 BC, many of which were memorialized by Pausanias. The Galatians, who were probably part of the Celtic people, were savage and strong fighters, but they committed terrible atrocities. They burned the ancient city of Callium to the ground and killed and abused its people. But the ancient Evrytanians, known as Aetolians, rallied and repelled the Galatians, who suffered many casualties. Especially instrumental were the brave women of Aetolia! The fierce battle took place in what is known today as Kokkalia, because of the many bones (in Greek, *kokkala*) still found in this area. The Aetolians fought and won an existential battle to save the entire Greek people, not just their civilization. As this book explains, if the Aetolians had lost, the Greek nation would have been lost.

Much has been learned from scattered archeological finds, legend, myths, and customs. Yet much remains to be learned. Accordingly, Mr. Fallis and Fr. Papademetriou both advocate for more excavation and research regarding this part of Greece, stating that this region has been severely under-studied. There is already much to be proud of, and further excavation and research will fill in our knowledge.

I. EVRYTANIA

"Happy is the one who studies one's history."
—*Euripides*

A Place with a Very Ancient History

It is certain and undoubtable that the history of Evrytania is great and very ancient, as is that of the rest of mainland Greece and the Greek islands. In certain periods in the history of Evrytania, the history is outrageous, and there is valuable information to be learned, yet we know very little. The paradox is that for all other ancient sites in Greece, efforts have been made, excavations have taken place, and many objects have been collected, enabling the writing of their history. For Evrytania, however, no such efforts have taken place. Its history remains a closed book; its history is buried. We have barely scratched the surface. For this reason, this small historical book serves to share at least the brief piece of history that is known to us today.

As we said, what we know is very minimal when compared with what we believe is the great treasure that is buried. We have collected this minimal evidence with great pain from scattered witnesses of the ancient authors, including Homer, Thucydides, Pausanias, Strabus, Tito Libius, and Polybius. There are also a few fragments of archaeology that have survived, which bear the message of the history of centuries before and after Christ. The Basilica at Klapsi (fifth century AD), built in the centuries after Christ, is a unique, historical, and religious monument of the Evrytanian province, which represents the traditions of the ancestors of Evrytania. The Basilica at Klapsi provides one of the visible links by which we hope to learn more about the important historical events of the centuries before Christ.

In the present volume, we will analyze and present the fragments of information that we have collected (the positions of ancient authors, findings, and traditions), until the time when full excavations can begin, to "open the page" — the page that is hidden today. In this book we will share what is known and bring to light areas where we can do further excavations, so as to see and learn more about our region's ineffable ancestral treasures. It is certain that the entire area of Evrytania is sown all over by very ancient cities, buried with their civilization — a civilization that is entirely unknown to us today. Someday, we will learn more fully about this and the role that this ancient civilization played in the historic development and the course of

Greek history. But for now, let us explore the areas we do know and bring to light the areas where further exploration and excavation can be done.

Buried Historical Treasure

If we compare history to a book, today we can only see the cover page of Evrytanian history. However, we are certain that in the closed volume there is a great treasure that remains to be discovered. Again, because vast areas of Evrytania remain neglected by archaeologists and have yet to be touched by archaeological excavations, we can only piece together the fragments of history that do exist. Although without full excavations these places remain silent, there are numerous castles and ancient burial settlements in Voulpi, Prasia, Tsouka, Palaiokantou, Kyfou, Lepiana, Mykrohrysou, Aroniada, Feidakia, Klapsi (or Klafsi), Koryskades,[1] Psiana, Fantinou, Kokkalia, and in many other areas throughout Evrytania. Indeed, it would be more accurate to state that there is not one corner of Evrytania that does *not* have a buried civilization and unrecognized history from the ancient age! In order to provide a foundation for this statement, in 1986 this author visited Kastanea and Tornos, villages in the south of Evrytania. The purpose of this visit was to see if there were already surface findings that confirmed the existence of an ancient civilization in Evrytania in the centuries before Christ. We were not surprised to conclude that there was indeed an ancient civilization. While there, our hands beheld fragments of ceramic jars of our classical age (fifth to fourth centuries BC). And this was not by any excavation or special effort.[2] We had the same experience at the location of Panagia of Krikello and at the location of Zaora, northeast of Kaliakouda. This confirmed for us that wherever one may step in Evrytania there remains hidden in the viscera of the earth an ancient and fascinating history which has been completely unknown to us. At around the same time, on June 28, 1987, as a bulldozer was opening a dirt road from Krikello to Domnista, about 1,500 meters from Krikello, the bulldozer uncovered a well-preserved stone tomb (length 1.2 m meters, width .80 meters) that was from the Geometric age (900-700 BC).[3] We speculate that the tomb is not the only tomb there, nor the most ancient in the area.

Evrytania is a boundless site of buried civilizations, with cities many layers underground, from the pre-mythical age to the long period of Turkish-imposed bondage. In this area there are buried civilizations, thousands of years old, with old and painful stories, which mark the way and make an unbroken connection with modern Greece. Each one of these castles, each fortress, and each tower holds a long unknown and unrecorded shocking history. What do we really know or could we write today in a few lines about the historical fortresses in Palaiokastro, which is northeast of Palaiokantou, with its enormous stones? And how can we record the history of the fortress on the hill of Tsouka, in which there are enclosed numerous acres, since the archaeological excavation has not reached this area?

It is interesting to note that this area still has the ancient name *"Hellenika,"*[4] which clearly shows that our roots are deep in history. We know that the originator of the Greek people, Hellene (Ελλην), is the son of Deucalion and Pyrrhus,[5] and Hellen created Greece in the neighboring south Thessaly in the mythical age, and spread his kingdom to the lands of Dolopon, Aperanton, Agraion, and Evrytanon. We say this yet again, but without excavation, how can we confirm if the remains of the ancient fortresses that exist in Viniani, in what is central Evrytania today, are not from the mythical and pre-mythical age? Even more so, who can go to Psiana, up to the village of Agia Paraskevi, "where there is a line of four square great stones indicating an ancient fortress?"[6] Who can go to show historically what people lived there, and what level of development of civilization existed in that period? When we go to the area of Fantinou of the community of Domnista, we now know in the ancient ages there existed a great civilization, but until recently, this city was completely unknown. It was discovered while digging to build a new road for the people to drive to the stables. By chance, this brought to light the Walls of Fantinou, walls built from large, chipped boulders but it is unknown to us how far they extended. Honestly, when will the systematic excavation in Evrytania begin, so we can learn more about our history in the real dimension, and we can share the pride of our land and its great contribution to Greek civilization?

[*Translator's Note: In the area of Petralona-Hohlia, Evrytania, on the mountain of Glas, an ancient statue of Dionysos was found in 1935. This statue is now housed in the National Archaeological Museum of Athens. There appears to have been an ancient center at this site. (Keramaris, Evripides and Vasileiou, Christos,* Petralona, Arahovitsa, Evrytanias *(Karpenisi, 2012), p. 17.)*]

Protachaioi, The First People Who Lived in Evrytania

It is impossible to know with absolute certainty in what time period Evrytania received its first inhabitants and from where these people may have come. We consider, however, as a historical certainty that in the pre-mythical period, as in the "Hellenic" era, there were various peoples who stopped in Evrytania, including the "First Achaeans," the "Pelasgians," the "Leleges," (aboriginal people before the Greeks arrived), and the "Kouretes" (Pre-Hellenic Aegean people before the Greeks arrived; *kouretes* means young men, young boys). We may never know with certainty which of these people first inhabited Evrytania. We consider most likely the first inhabitants of the Evrytaniko-Aetoliko area were the "First Achaeans," who displaced or absorbed the few inhabitants who might have been there prior to the Achaeans coming. The "First Achaeans" were driven out from Thessaly and were established in the area around Aetolia by the River Acheloos. Over time, however, they expanded to the nearby area of present-day Evrytania. These people were known as "Achaeans," the same people who later came into alliance with other Greek peoples, the Aetolians. It was this group that made up the military group of Achaeans who overthrew the Pelasgians[7] from Thessaly. Again, before the First Achaeans there were likely other peoples who stopped and found refuge in the vast mountainous forests of Evrytania. It is important that Professor Theodore Havellas points out that, "Historically, certainly, it is considered that these peoples came down from Asia to Thessaly, and from there they spread first to Aetolia and Akarnania, however there the Lapithons, a people from Thessaly, pushed these peoples back."[8]

It seems that these peoples were then absorbed with the passing of time by the First Achaeans. These peoples, both the First Achaeans and the unmingled inhabitants of these areas, became the first permanent inhabitants.

We do not know for certain what name was given for this area at that time. But later, from the Homeric period on, this area was known as the nation of Evrytos, or Evrytania. Here, we must take seriously the position of the great tragedian-poet Sophocles (fifth century BC), who refers to ΤΡΑΧΙΝΙΕΣ *(The Women of Trachinies)*,[9] and makes reference to the land of Evrytos: " 'Evrytos and his high tower Oechalia' were destroyed."[10] It is evident that Evrytania, prior to the time of Evrytos, during his time, and until his death, was called "Evryteia." This is an important fact for the history of ancient Evrytania. Unfortunately, we do not have exact elements from our far distant ancestors to help us to know with certainty who developed the area of Evrytania during this particular millennium.

The Earliest People in Evrytania

Despite not knowing with certainty who the earliest peoples were, with the seriousness and persistence of observing the area of the bygone millennia, we may come to a conclusion that Evrytania was indeed inhabited five thousand years ago. It is true that Evrytania has not done any excavations to confirm this speculation. However, there are some objects at the Karpenisi Public Library (i.e. various small findings from the middle Greek Civilization (1900-1600 BC)) that were gathered from the area of Agios Demetrios in Evrytania.

During this period, when the human population increased, the peoples sought to live in uninhabited lands so as to offer to their families and herds safety in accordance with the nomadic rules of their tribes. Evrytania had all the resources to support these first peoples in a way and in a condition to live well during that period. In the boundless forests there was a variety of abundant hunting. Also, there were unlimited grazing areas in Evrytania, and numerous rivers and ravines, with crystal clear running water.

Evrytania became a magnet for those people who wished to live a simple life, far from cities, far from raids by foreign enemies, far from massacres that caused a destruction of people and their flocks. In Evrytania the people could live a safe life. They could cultivate everything in the valleys and slopes of the mountains without any privation. Evrytania was indeed a refuge for the first people of the area, especially the area by the river that provided a means to survive. In those years, Evrytania was self-sufficient in all the goods needed to live a good life. Such a land was Evrytania.

The Language

The first tribes and generally the first people who inhabited the mountainous area of Evrytania were from the pre-mythical period. It appears that they did not develop an evil tendency to mutually exterminate each other as in other areas. They had developed the spirit of cooperation and made every effort to unite so they could live in peace and in creativity together.[11] The unity and peace they developed with other people would ultimately prove to be very beneficial to help them face the invaders and plunderers who eventually came there.

We are not able today to know details, the way of life, and the specific historical development of this area. Furthermore, we are not able to know the habits and customs of that time. We do not know which Pelasgian dialect they spoke, what gods they worshiped, and what level of civilization the people brought from their place of origin. Nevertheless, it is certain that these inhabitants, with the passing of time, not only got used to inhabiting this area, but they adjusted, and adapted to the environment of this land. They loved this land and bonded with it. Thus, they lived in that way in isolation, closed in by the wild mountainous environment. They adopted from this their wild and hard character.

This environment and the way of life compelled the people to create closed characters, unyielding—when necessary. They did this to protect themselves from whatever would harm them and their area, their family, or diminish and tarnish their human dignity. The Evrytanians stood strong in the passing of thousands of years with their local customs, with their strange and rough uncompromised character, their own customs and manners, and their own incomprehensible—to other people—language up to the historical age.

Basically, the ancient Evrytanian language was that of the Aetolians-Dorians.[12] Through the ages, the Evrytanians preserved their ancient language.[13] That is why Thucydides (fifth century BC) writes, "Evrytanians, of whom the greater part belong to the Aetolians, have an incomprehensible language and they eat raw foods."[14] Theodore Havellas provides us with important information regarding the language of the ancient Aetolians. He states, "According to Polybius, the historian who flourished around the second Macedonian war, the Aetolians had the same language and were of the same people of Arkananon and Macedonians. However, according to Strabo, around the first century after Christ, in the area around Oxylon, Aetolians in the most ancient times spoke the same language as the Eleiois after the descent of the Herakledon. From all the surviving witnesses and from the surviving words and names, especially Aetolian Branstaiteros, their writing was primarily related to that of the Aetolians and the Dorians."[15]

[*Translator's Note: The Evrytanians were admired with great respect for their generosity and bravery—virtues that were very important for the ancient Greeks. Evrytania was a great nation (ethnos) well versed in the martial arts.*]

Religious Life in Ancient Evrytania

In those times it is certain that religion was of innate importance to all human beings. It was a way of life. For that reason, from the beginning of the appearance of human beings on earth, religion was beneficial as a refuge and support, and it became a factor in progress and civilization. In the early age of human creation, in which humans were in immediate relation with their God-Creator, they felt safe and without suffering. After the disobedience of God's commandment, however, humans were distanced from their Creator-Father, found themselves lost, unprotected, and exposed to the law of corruption. This only increased with the passage of time, when people multiplied on all the earth. At the same time, in order to survive, the people had to familiarize themselves with nature, and to face the ferocity of nature, such as earthquakes and floods. They had to face the danger of beasts, as well as the plagues and famine that beat them down, the unbearable psychological and physical pain, and, ultimately death, which led them each time to depression. For that reason, they had a need for protection—somewhere to find refuge, to alleviate their dreadful sufferings. However, the disobedience of God's commandment clouded their minds and the way to return to their Creator-Father was lost. Thus, only a few, with difficulty, sought and found refuge in God. The majority of the people were dispersed to the ends of the earth, creating in accordance with their situation, gods made from the elements of nature. These peoples offered their gods sacrifices, praying for propitiation, and praying to feel safe under the protection of their gods.

The Evrytanians, in the Neolithic age when they first inhabited Evrytania, also brought with them from their place of origin their religious foundation. We do not know what gods they worshipped at that time and their way of worship. We do not know how and how often they expressed their worship. That which we are certain of is that they had a religion that they practiced to support them up until the mythical age. The information that we have in our possession comes from a later period. It is from the mythical period, when there was an increase and combining of the populations. According to the consensus of scholarly opinion, the Evrytanians worshipped the same gods as the rest of the Greek world. Parallel to the Greek pantheon, the Evrytanians created their own gods or deified their heroes and, as time went on, they created similar religious rituals. It is certain that these ancestors of long ago were pious people.

In this pious behavior, the Evrytanians made every effort, even in the mythical age, to invite all the nation-tribes, to unite peacefully, and to live as a nation as one political and military power with the rest of the Greeks. For that reason, the Oracle of Odysseus was not for them only a place of worship, or a shrine, but especially a place that united all the Greeks in their worship. "The Evrytanian nation, had a shrine[16] where Odysseus was worshipped, and a memorable shrine preserved from an ancient age received this practice of the worship of Odysseus." "They were most pious and respectful toward the divinities, the common gods of the Greeks, honoring mostly Apollo, Athena, Artemis, Demetra, and Dionysus. They built temples in numerous places in Aetolia in the cities or outside the cities. They had religious celebrations, similar to the rest of the Greeks, the most prominent was that of the Thalysia, for the fertility of the fruits of the earth, as a thanksgiving to all the gods."[17]

That the Evrytanians were pious people and had built numerous temples is witnessed by the ancient historians. We will make a few references here, such as the ancient historian Pausanias, who writes about the invasion of the ancient city of Callium by the Galatians in the year 279 BC. Pausanias says, "As the barbarians plunder the homes and the holy places and set fire to the Callium..."[18] We see here that the Evrytanians, in the third century BC had in their capital sacred places or shrines, that is, many temples. This was a tradition for the Evrytanians that they continued in the subsequent generations to the time of the coming of Christianity (see Dem.

Fallis, *Kallion Evrytanias*, pp. 107-124). Thus, Christianity, for the Evrytanians, was corrective in their journey of faith toward their God-Creator, the God of revelation, and for this reason they accepted Christianity immediately. There are a number of historical references from the first Christians. We especially have the great tangible proof, the Church of Agios Leonides of Klapsi, built in the fifth century AD, which I will discuss below.

The Boundaries of Ancient Evrytania

The present boundaries of the eparchy of Evrytania are different from the boundaries of ancient times. The present area of Evrytania was fixed following the victory of the struggle of the modern nation of Greece in 1821 and the liberation from the Turks.[19] In ancient times, the boundaries were around the mountain of Tymphristos in the north, and in the south to the mountain Aetoliko.[20] In order to determine the area of ancient Evrytania during the pre-historical period of 3000 BC and the post-Helladic period of 1600-1100 BC, we need to consult the ancient and modern writers. We know that through the centuries and millennia the population of Evrytania increased, pressured by the neighboring tribes, sometimes the boundaries were limited, and other times expanded. The author K.D. Stergiopoulos in his book, *Ancient Aetolia*, writes, "When the Evrytanians were a large population, their borders expanded to where today is the River Krikelioton, having as a boundary the River Euenon, the mountain Tymphristos, the present-day Megdoban, and looking out in the west the rising mountains of Aetolia toward the valley of Agrinion."[21] These fluctuations of Evrytania's borders continued up to the ancient period.

The Expansion of the Boundaries of Evrytania

Around the ancient period (700-480 BC), it appears that Evrytania expanded its boundaries a little more, especially in the northwest. The Evrytanian author, Panos Vasileiou, writes:

> From the fifth century BC and after, Evrytania included the area of the Evrytanians, Arakynthion, Karpenision, and Parakampylion, with neighbors in the north the Dolopes, to the east the Ainianes, to the west the Aperantous, to the south the Thestieis, and to the south the Aetolous, and to the northwest the Ophioneis. The boundaries of south and southwest are not easy to define with precision because it is said that at times the boundaries reached the banks of the Lake of Trichonidas, which includes the Thermon and Agrinion.[22]

That which is considered certain, however, is that the center of Evrytania from ancient times to the historical period BC, was in Potamia, which extends south of Tymphristos. This is due to the fact that Potamia had the most suitable land to create residential areas and cities, especially capital cities, and because it was the most fruitful area in Evrytania. For that reason, in Potamia great cities were created and a great local original civilization was developed, even in the prehistoric and mythical times and lasted under the myriad challenges and destructions up to the fifteenth century AD, when Evrytania was captured and enslaved by the Turks under Murat II (the sixth Turkish Sultan ca. 1404-1451).[23]

II. EVRYTOS
HISTORY—LEGEND (THRYLLOS)

"Evrytania is a nation of Aetolia that was named after its founder Evrytos."
—Lycophron (fourth century BC)

The Originator of the Evrytanians

According to the information we have, we consider that Evrytos was a historical person who lived before the mythical period. That is the period of which we have no concrete written information. It is certain that in the pre-mythical period when Evrytos lived, there were written words on stones, metals, or on wood, but with very little circulation. This was the time when communication was by oral word. And the instruction of the arts and the instruction of vocation or business basically was done orally, by experience, with the apprenticeship of the pupil.

We hope that in the near future there will be archaeological excavations in Evrytania, in the areas where Evrytos lived, where he reigned and became "Evrytos the Great."[24] Perhaps the findings that will come to light will include stones and metals with written words of that time. Today, we have as sources of information mythology and local traditions. Both of these sources need special attention and critical study for one to come to the true conclusion and to learn the historical truth.

The mythical period of Evrytania extends to two thousand years before Christ. The historical events that are mentioned are enriched with poetic and imaginary elements of local traditions to connect the events of ancient times. However local traditions have weakened with the passing of time, keeping untouched only the seed of the truth of the events. Therefore, we cannot accept either of these sources, neither the mythology nor the local traditions, without discernment as historical sources, and at the same time we cannot completely reject them without analyzing them to accept them as truth. Both hold historical truth and weight as appropriate in the course of human life. First, let us examine the mythology.

Legend

As mentioned before, the legendary period of Evrytania covered the period of two thousand years before Christ. However, for the prior years, life and civilization were in constant flux and development, and we do not have concrete written information of anything prior. Starting in the mythical age, many ancient authors wrote according to the period that they lived and the sources they had.

The first and the greatest author of the mythical age was Homer. In his two immortal, classical works, the *Iliad* and the *Odyssey*, Homer preserved the most important intellectual information for humanity. Many ancient writers borrowed from Homer regarding the mythical age. However, the *Iliad* and the *Odyssey* were stories, and for historians they lacked historical truth, until the time of Heinrich Schliemann. The myths and poetry of Homer's imagination resounded to the "audience of the upper class that regarded the Homeric heroes as their ancestors."[25] In 1875 and after, the insistence and excavation of one who was not an expert but an admirer of ancient archaeology, namely Heinrich Schliemann, uncovered the mythological archaeological treasures of the ancient city of Troy in Asia Minor. The literary problem for the first time became a historical problem. According to Wilamowitz-Moellendorff, "The faith having become historical, Homer now transposes the mountains, the rivers, and the islands."[26] Wilamowitz-Moellendorff continues, "Thus Homer must occupy a place in the historical development. We are certain that by further research in the depths of Asia Minor many more surprises will be found. That is, the legends of the heroes included in the epics, which survived to our time by the local traditions, do not completely lack some historical truth in the content, in spite of the poetic literary liberty taken by poetic genius."[27]

Tradition

The other source of information about the past is tradition. This tradition not only informs us of the historical existence of Evrytos, but also tells us of the location where he reigned, lived, and left a mark of his grandeur. Before we state the local tradition about Evrytos, we must clarify here that we do not talk about "the mythical stories that we believe as facts,"[28] as Nick Polites writes. This is because not even a fairytale from the past passed to us today. We are talking about "a collective event of the past, even if that event may have been lost in the night of a time long ago," as the philosopher Emanuel Kant very well speaks about.[29]

We are talking about a tradition that has its roots deep in time that is able to function today and construct the future; such a tradition that was not disrupted from the historical event by the passing of time. There are villages in Evrytania that tell the story of their legendary king, Evrytos. This is especially true in the villages in the area of Potamia and the villages of southeast Evrytania such as Psiana, Domnista, Syggrelo, Stabloi, and others, which still claim this tradition. The village Stabloi especially, which had the privilege of being known as the place where Evrytos kept his stables, would not change its name.[30]

This living tradition helped preserve to the present-day the belief that Evrytos was a real person and lived and did great deeds in this place that we call Evrytania. This was at the same time and in conjunction with the traditions and the witness of the ancient writers who make reference to Evrytania. Some ancient writers refer to Evrytos as indeed existing and as King of Oechalia and originator of the Evrytanians!

One of those ancient writers was Lycophron (fourth century BC) who writes, "Aristotle stated in his work, *Ithakesion Politeia*, that: 'Evrytania is a nation of Aetolia and was named by Evrytos.'"[31]

Also, Theodore Havellas in his work, *History of the Aetolians*, states that, "Regarding the Evrytanians, especially from the witness of Aristotle and Nikandros, we are informed that Evrytania received its name from the famous hero Evrytos."[32]

The Origin of Evrytos

Present-day researchers as well as classical historical writers, both the ancient and modern writers who seriously studied the mythical and pre-mythical times, lead us to the conclusion that Evrytos existed and was the son of Melaneas and Oechalia.[33] Melaneas was considered the son of Apollo and was the king of Dryopon. Dryopon was an ancient people who lived in mainland Greece before the arrival of the first Greeks.[34] These were the first inhabitants of the ancient region of Doris, who dispersed all the way to the valley of Spercheios. [*Translator's note: Doris [pronounced Dor-ís] is the name used by English-speaking classics scholars for this Ancient*

Greek region. In Greece today, a province covering this area is known as Dorida.] The Dryopes were displaced later by the Dorians who created four cities in Doris: those were Kytinion, Erineon, Boion, and Pindon or Akyfanta.[35] The Dryopes, displaced from Doris, settled in other areas of Greece such as Euboea, Kythno, Ermione, and in various areas of Peloponnesos.

Evrytos was a real human being endowed with a great number of virtues. He was intelligent, brave, bold, and venturesome. With these talents and with a combination of being a royal descendant, he was destined to be the most glorious king of his time. He began and organized a nation, the people of Evrytania, and a civilization of a great level that continued in later ages of the mythical age, and which we later get to know in the historical age and the age of the glorious Aetolian Commonwealth. The fame of Evrytos reached to Thrace (Iliad β'595) as "GREAT EVRYTOS."

For many centuries, his name became a symbol of courage and an example in the art of war for the youth. He created the Kingdom of Evrytania by uniting small nations and organized it in an exemplary way for that time. He created the capital city of Oechalia, named to honor his mother's name. He also created other cities and centers in many areas of his kingdom, and appointed the local leaders and stable managers to manage his great estate with thousands of cows and unnumbered herds of goats and sheep. Many researchers of the ancient texts interpret that Evrytos was the inventor of the bow.[36] Perhaps this is not true. One thing is true: that Evrytos was an excellent archer. According to Apollodoros, Evrytos instructed even Heracles in the use of the bow.[37] Evrytos was such a good archer and confident in his marksmanship that he even challenged "the immortals," that is Apollo, to a duel. And one story says that this resulted in Evrytos being killed by Apollo in a duel. We hear the following verses stated by Odysseus in the *Odyssey*:

> Evrytos of Oechalia, a hero who vied with gods in bowmanship. Evrytos came to grief, it's true; old age never crept over him in his long hall; Apollo took his challenge ill, and killed him.[38]

However, another story says that Evrytos, abandoned by Apollo, was killed by Heracles, because Evrytos placed himself above the immortals and challenged the gods to a duel. For his excessive ego, mortal Evrytos could not be left unpunished by the gods. Evrytos of Oechalia, who strove even with the immortals in archery, must be punished. Therefore, great Evrytos died early; old age did not come upon him in his halls. In the story with Heracles, here we also have the true witness of Apollodoros,[39] that Evrytos proclaimed an archery contest and promised to give as the prize the most beautiful girl, Evrytos's daughter, Iole. In this contest, the victor was Heracles, and Evrytos broke his word and did not give Iole to be Heracles's bride because Evrytos was afraid that Heracles would murder her offspring as he had done to the children that he had with another wife, Megara. This act of denying Iole to Heracles destroyed Evrytos and his kingdom because Evrytos was killed by the angry Heracles. Thus, Oechalia was completely destroyed. Many of the ancient writers record this shocking event of the murder of Evrytos and the destruction of Oechalia. Let us here make reference only to Sophocles in *The Women of Trachinies*:

> I myself heard this man say,
> while many were present,
> who witnessed the girl [of Iole],
> Heracles destroyed Evrytos
> and his high-towered Oechalia.[40]

Oechalia

Those who are occupied with the research in the historical place of Evrytania—even a very little bit—know that Oechalia carries an immediate, continued relation with the person of Evrytos because he was the founder and king of the city of Oechalia, which he named after his mother. According to ancient writers and some modern interpreters, we have six Oechalias at various places of Greece.[41]

"Oechalia, city of Thessaly at the Peneiou, seat of Evrytos, however there were other cities, in Messenia near Arkadia, Kairnasion, Euboia, Trachinia, and Aetolia."[42]

This does not seem possible. What does it mean that there were six cities of Oechalias but one Evrytos? Of which Oechalia was Evrytos the founder and king?

The First Oechalia

We know that there have been no excavations in Evrytania so that we can see what buried kingships might reveal historical surprises. Even so, our research will continue to discover every possible written source that will give us the correct—historical—answer regarding the place of King Evrytos. Thus, as we have researched and written[43] elsewhere, Evrytos existed and was the founder and king who founded the fortified city that he named Oechalia in honor of his mother. This was the FIRST Oechalia. The other Oechalias were founded later by the dispersed people who carried with them the history and glory of the FIRST Oechalia[44] following the horrible destruction of Oechalia by the enraged Heracles. "Heracles destroyed Evrytos and his high-towered Oechalia."[45] Also, we know that the first Oechalia was in the area of the ancient Evrytania[46] and specifically in the area of Potamias. For these reasons, there are many witnesses by ancient and modern authors, although it is impossible to enumerate all of them here. However, it is helpful to make reference to some of these authors in order for us to form a vision of the existence and place of the first Oechalia.

Strabo (67 BC-23 AD), who is the most important geographer of the ancient world, writes, "There is also a village Oechalia in the remains of the city that was destroyed by Heracles: it bears the same name as the Trachinia and the Arkadiki of Andanian which the people of later times called Aetolia and was in the territory of Evrytania."[47]

We see here that Strabo places ancient Evrytania within the general area of Aetolia. It is clear that he establishes the existence of Oechalia within the small—at that time—area of Evrytania. This reference to Evrytania by Strabo confirms for that we do not need to search for Oechalia elsewhere. For this reason, on the chart-map published in Paris by Guillermo Delisle (1707), Oechalia is placed on the left bank of the Acheloos River,[48] that is, within the area of Evrytania. Furthermore, in a map of Greece created by Fr. Miller in 1797 in Vienna, Miller placed Oechalia north of Agrinion.[49] For that reason from 1833–1840[50] the eparchy of Evrytania was called the eparchy of Kallidromes, and at one time Karpenisi was called Oechalia, "to connect it with the ancient capital city of Evrytania, the city of Evrytos."[51]

Oechalia at Klapsi

For the exact location of Oechalia within Evrytania, we have many views by the contemporary researchers and historians that place it in several places: Fedakia,[52] Hohlia, on the mount

Kombolos in Domianous, in Koryskades, or in Klapsi. According to the results of our research, we believe that Oechalia was located in Potamia of the present-day Klapsi. We could make reference to numerous authors who support our view. We will make only two references: to the Evrytanian historians Panos Vasileiou and Athanasios Iatrides. Vasileiou, in his book, *Villages of Evrytania that were Destroyed*, writes, "It is possible the Klapsi of today was the capital city of ancient Evrytania with another name, if it had not the name of Oechalia."[53] Even more clear and convincing about the location of Oechalia in Klapsi is Athanasios Iatrides, who writes:

On the topic of the name of Oechalia, there were several locations inhabited by ancient Greeks but disappeared from time immemorial, due to the fact that it is far from the city of Karpenisi: a distance of about two hours south, and we found numerous chips of broken earthen jars and tiles, and traces of a square ancient wall, in addition above Klapsi on the eastern side of the village an ancient fortress and gold and copper coins, on the one hand they have Macedonian inscriptions, and on the other hand by the Aetolian in Roman inscriptions and are the last of the Greek decline, by which sign one could believe that here was the ancient Oechalia.[54]

In parallel to this historical evidence, we must also emphasize that this location called Potamia is the present Klapsi. This confirms the presupposition that the capital city founded by King Evrytos was in ancient Evrytania. This is because: a) Klapsi was the geographic center of Evrytania, and the king could best exercise control of all the kingdom and have speedy communications with his subjects, and b) more importantly, Klapsi was near sufficient tillable land and abundant water to irrigate this land. There were two rivers (the Karpenisioti and Mouzelioti) and two great inexhaustible gushing springs. These springs gush even today in the northeast and south of Klapsi. Thus, we consider it certain that Oechalia, "Evrytos's City," survived numerous destructions and challenges in the prehistoric ages (eighth to seventh centuries BC). To this day we do not know what developments and changes happened that caused this place to be named Callium. Now, nothing else remains, except the necessity to commence the archaeological digging as soon as possible in Klapsi so as to bring to light the parallel buried cities of the Byzantine era and of the Roman times; the city of Callium, which was destroyed by the Galatians in 279 BC; and the city of Oechalia of Evrytos, which was destroyed by Heracles.

The Oracle of Odysseus

Without a doubt, the famous "Oracle of Odysseus" was an institution that played an important role in the spiritual and cultural development of Evrytania. However, there are some writers who doubted that the Oracle of Odysseus, this great religious and cultural center, was in Evrytania. Perhaps these writers were ill-informed, or they intentionally distorted the facts because the Evrytanians were "different from the rest of the Greeks, for they were uncivilized."[55] In the *Great Greek Encyclopedia*, P. Drandakes writes, "The most impossible thing is to believe that the mountainous people from their reading of the Odyssey were moved to honor the hero by worshipping, by consulting him as a soothsayer."[56] Apparently, these writers refused to examine in depth the history of Evrytania and to see the facts without bias, and that the particular Evrytanian original civilization and the spiritual development of the Evrytanians of that time were viewed this way because the contemporaries were jealous of them. It is telling that the Oracle of Odysseus in Evrytania was referenced by the prominent scholar Is. I. Tzetses, Leipsia 1811, in his commentary on Lycophron, a fragment from Aristotle's "Ithakeia Politeia." Aristotle states: "Evrytanes, a nation of the Aetolians that was named thus by Evrytos, the place of the Oracle of Odysseus."[57] And Lycophron (fourth century BC), the ancient poet who was a descendant from Chalkida, in his difficult to understand poem, *Alexandra or Cassandra*, writes, "The people crowned the soothsayer Evrytos."[58] Theodore Havellas confirmed the place of the Oracle of Odysseus in Evrytania in his wonderful book, *History of the Aetolians*. Havellas writes, "The Evrytanian nation had special adoration of Odysseus and his memorable Oracle survived from the ancient times and certainly received these traditions."[59]

Precise Location of the Oracle of Odysseus

The precise location of the Oracle of Odysseus within the boundaries of ancient Evrytania remains unknown. All the writers who were occupied with the Oracle of Odysseus conjecture that it existed in northern Evrytania and precisely at the "Great Cave of Apokleistra in the area of Kastanea." Kostas Mpaltas from Kastanea refers to K.S. Konsta, who writes in the *Aetoloakarnanike kai Evrytanike Enkyclopedia*, the following, "We may conjecture that in the ancient times this cave was the place of the Oracle honoring the name of the Homeric Odysseus."[60] We do not know when this conjecture became prevalent, but these writers never visited this place to have a personal experience and position.

In the summer of 1986, I visited Kastanea and the next day the cave Apokleistra. Our goal was to collect elements that would be helpful to us to confirm that the Oracle of Odysseus was in this cave called "Great Apokleistra." Sometime in the future we will return to deal specifically with details regarding this place of Apokleistra. At present, however, we must exclude every conjecture that the Oracle of Odysseus may have been located in this "cave."

Evrytos — History — Legend

The impossibility of the Oracle of Odysseus being located at the cave, Great Apokleistra, is supported by the researcher from that area of Kastanea, Zacharias Zeveles. In his handwritten notes, which we have, Zeveles states the following, "The fact that this cave is a place not easily accessible convinces us that the Oracle of Odysseus could not have been located there." In reality, this location is not a cave but a great ravine both internally and externally—an opening in the steep rocks—a ravine that makes it practically impossible for man or animal to go there because it is dangerous.

Therefore, the location of the Oracle of Odysseus remains an open issue. The research continues, however, and we are convinced that the Oracle will be discovered. We are convinced that the location of the Oracle of Odysseus was in the region of southern ancient Evrytania. This region of southern Evrytania had a civilization from very ancient times and was the only way connecting, from the Neolithic age, Thessaly through Evrytania and Mount Panaetolikon, with Thermo and generally Aetolia. Thucydides says, "The Aetolian nation was great and with great warriors."

The Aetolian Commonwealth

One of the most important achievements, if not the greatest in the passing of time, is the Aetolian Commonwealth—a historical chapter that is almost unknown. Unfortunately, there has not been serious research nor studies in an objective way with "historical passion" to collect written and physical elements. There has not been a more comparative and organized study of the long duration of the ancient world. The formation of the Aetolian Commonwealth has not been repeated even today. This type of political system is very ancient, rooted in the mythical period. Unfortunately, this region has been neglected by the archaeological excavation from the time of our independence from the Turks until today. After Greek independence from the Turks, some Greek politicians from other regions usurped the national fortunes and the national claims and pushed out the Evrytanian fighters and heroes of 1821 to a slow death, some begging for bread in the streets. As if this were not enough, in addition they distorted and falsified the Evrytanian history, and they presented the Evrytanians as without ancient history, savages, and uncivilized, who lived by "robbery and plundering." As an example, we shall present a historical example of this slandering of the Aetolians. Due to the lack of time and space, we shall make reference to only one, Sp. P. Lambros, who writes:

> Since the other cities and other people of Greece were advanced in civilization, they were distinguished by their activities. The Aetolians lived a life in which the major part of their land was mountainous, they were al-

ways armored, and they were different from the rest of the Greeks, for they were uncivilized. However, after the times of Alexander the Great, the people came out from many centuries of dullness and appeared suddenly to be active among the other Greeks. Even after this luminous period of the Aetolians, in the last analysis of the tragedy of the ancient Greek world immediately after the destruction does not change its character from the prior way of life. The people were armored as in the olden days and elevated this way of life into a system. And behaved by devastation and continuous warfare. This is the new history of the Aetolians. Regarding education, art, intellectual formation and higher civilization there is nothing to be said about these. The only necessary art for them was fortification, and the only vital virtue was bravery. From their cities, or rather their villages, were forts that were closed when they were not mobilizing to go out to devastate and rob. The only new element that they introduced in the way of life of the Aetolians during this time was the political unity as a result of necessity and the danger they faced during the Lamian War. All the tribes of Aetolia were united in 322 BC to face the enemy.[61]

Unification of the Aetolians in 322 BC

It is not possible to make a full commentary of the entire story of Evrytos. I have written more about this in the newspaper *"Evrytania,"* (in the sections numbered 19, 21, and 27-28). The reader may read the commentary to judge for themselves how ridiculous the statement by Lambros is and to draw their own conclusion. Here, since we make reference to the Aetolian Commonwealth, we will comment on the last line of Lambros's statement, "United—the Aetolians—in 322 BC." There are numerous witnesses from ancient writers and even contemporary writers that prove that Lambros's statements are historically unfounded as to the date of the Aetolian unification. We shall refer to some. And first of all, the only position of the greatest and most objective historian of ancient times, Thucydides, who personally experienced the attack of the Athenian General Demosthenes (426 BC), and his allies against the Aetolians, writes:

> The Aetolians, he explained, that were, it was true, a great and warlike people, but as they lived in unwalled villages, which, moreover, were widely separated, and as they used light armor, they could be subdued without difficulty before they could unite for mutual defense. And they advised him to attack Apodoton first, then the Ophioneans, and after them, the Evrytanians. These last constitute the largest division of the Aetolians, their speech is more unintelligible than the other Aetolians, and according to the report, they are eaters of raw flesh. If these tribes were subdued, they said, the rest would readily yield.[62]

We are certain that this position of Thucydides is catalytic to the position of Lambros. Thucydides was the first to record the unification of the Aetolian tribes into one nation in the fifth century BC that included the Apodotoi, the Ophioneis, and the Evrytanians. The Aetolian Commonwealth existed before 322 BC. Herman Bengtson, in his book, *Istoria tes Archaias Ellados* (*History of Ancient Greece*), writes, "The Commonwealth of the Aetolians was mentioned for the first time in an Athenian inscription that dates to 367 BC." Bengtson's position is very significant not just because this inscription is dated before 322 BC, but also because the inscription is Athenian.[63]

The academician K.A. Romaios states: "In the political history of the Aetolians, they appeared united for the first time in 426 BC when they defended against the Athenian Demosthenes and repulsed them. It is not, however, correct that this was the first time that they came to recognize their tribal relationship and their common interests." And K.A. Romaios continues: "In reality as is evident in these places references are made in the prehistoric period and after the Aetolians found a Commonwealth stretched throughout their mountainous wilderness. This did not compel by force by the stronger tribes but by the recognition of the common interest."[64]

From the Mythical Times

As we mentioned in the beginning of this

chapter, this political formation of the Aetolians is rooted "in the very depth of time, reaching back to the mythical age." And this is very important. This is the result of a very careful and serious study of the ancient texts. Ever since the time of Evrytos, these tribes "were conscious of their tribal relationship and their common intent." And for that reason, they made every effort not to engage in rivalry and destructive warfare among each other. They strove to unite as one political and military power, as one nation, the nation of the Aetolians. Each tribe and each nationality in this Commonwealth developed its own political physiognomy and particularity. This particularity was preserved in the following centuries until the historical age "when they appeared for the first time uniting and acting together in 426 BC." This was what created the unity and the peaceful coexistence among these people. In the book by Theodore Havellas, *Istoria Ton Aetolon (History of the Aetolians)*, we read:

> The history of the Aetolian nation extended to all Aetolia such that it necessitated a representative be sent to Lacedaemon and Corinth from further off tribes. This points out that the ancient Aetolians and the Epiktetou Apodotoi, Ophioneis, Evrytanians and the rest of the Aetolians collaborated against the invasion of the Athenians, and this collaboration of the Aetolians proves the unification of the Aetolian nation that was solidified later into the organiza-

tion that formed the Aetolian Commonwealth.[65]

And Havellas continues:

> The Commonwealth of Aetolia has its beginnings as a type of political system since the Homeric age when the Aetolians appeared as one solid nation. This type of Aetolian Commonwealth is about: Each city-state and the bond of the Commonwealth is independent. The same ruler of the alliance treated independently, the Aetolians and the rest of the members of the Commonwealth, without any privilege or discrimination and sovereignty. Issues of war and peace and negotiation of treaties were done by an assembly representing from all the States of the Commonwealth. The internal governance of each state must be free to govern its own affairs, and if possible, each state is to have common council to govern and mandate the affairs of the state.[66]

It is obvious from the ancient texts that the Aetolians "were different from the rest of the Hellenes for they were uncivilized," which was wrongly presented by Lambros. Historically, the Aetolian Commonwealth was created in 426 BC and not 322 BC, and we must emphasize that it had its origin much earlier—it was a created period but developed through the centuries. It was not a collaboration of some tribes to face the danger of the time, but a family of tribes that collaborated to make their common interest to move forward as a nation. It was a commonwealth of all the tribes "without privileges and discriminations." The rules were equally valid for all the cities and individuals. And this was unprecedented not only for the ancient world but even in our contemporary "civil" society. And for that reason, it lasted for many centuries. The Commonwealth held for such a long period of time: from the ancient times to 146 BC when it was subjected to the Romans after a hard fight and became a senatorial province of Macedonia under the Romans.

III. CALLIUM

Translator's Note: The author Demetrios Fallis argues in this chapter that the ancient city of Callium was located in present-day Klapsi of Evrytania, and not elsewhere in Greece, and in particular not in Velouchovo in the ancient region of Doris. This is important for Greek and Evrytanian history because Callium was an important capital city in ancient times. (Callium is the name used by English-speaking classics scholars; in Greek, Callium is called Kallipolis or Kallion.) Callium was destroyed by the ancient Galatians, but it was also the place from where the Aetolians (another name for the ancient Evrytanians) fought bravely and repelled the Galatians, thus saving the Greek nation from extinction in 279 BC. These battles and events will be described in the next chapter regarding Kokkalia.

In the Wrong Location

We think that it is difficult to recount accurately the history of a glorious city that existed so long ago in time. This is true of the city of Callium. However, in the case of the city of Callium, it is even more difficult to recount its history because of a historical mistake made by the Greek government. In 1915,[67] the Greek Ministry of Internal Affairs issued a document, imposing a stop to research ancient Callium further by giving the city two names: Kallipolis and Callium.

This author, Demetrios Fallis, addresses this mistake in a long period of research. He researched two places—the region of Doris and the region of Evrytania—to confirm this historical mistake. He published on it in 1982 in his book, *Kallion Evrytanias, A New View of the History of Callium*. In this book, author Fallis based his position on the tradition of Klapsi, a municipalilty in Evrytania (also known as Klafsi), and the surrounding villages. The research focused on the objects of ancient civilizations that were found spread throughout the region of Evrytania. There was also research by the ancient historians such as Thucydides and Pausanias. Fallis confirmed that ancient Callium, which was completely destroyed by the Galatians in 279 BC, did not exist in Doris, in the municipality of the Velouchovo, but in Evrytania itself, in the municipality of Klapsi. Author I.M. Chazephotis writes, "Until archaeological excavation in Klapsi and Kokkalia elucidates in a systematic way, fully illuminating the matter, it is not possible to overturn the theory of Demetrios Fallis."[68] Regarding Velouchovo, as Demetrios Fallis writes, we do not have any findings of any ancient objects in Velouchovo to indicate that

Callium 67

the city of Callium was located there. This is despite the fact that archaeological excavations were held in Velouchovo in 1977-1979. They did not find any archaeological objects, or historical facts, or any local tradition, to indicate that Callium was located in Velouchovo.

Without any evidence, other historians have responded to Mr. Fallis's arguments with the answer that: "We inform you that ancient Callium has been found and has been researched by archaeological digging. It is located in the village of Velouchovo."[69] Nevertheless, we have here presented a summary of the long history of ancient Callium, in order for each reader to form their own view on the location of Callium, for the glory of this city, a glory that encompasses all of the land of Evrytania!

The Contemporary View Regarding Callium

Many contemporary Greek historians repeat, without critical and deep investigation, the mistaken view of George Soteriades that ancient Callium was located in Doris. This mistake began in 1907 when Soteriades circulated his historical study in Paris. Soteriades's study commences, without foundation, the creation of an enormous historical structure by Greek and foreign historians and archaeologists. Thus, to this day, important historical and school textbooks in geography, maps of our homeland, the encyclopedias, and even the monumental publication of *History of the Greek Nation*, v. 15, Athens, 1970-1978),[70] repeat the mistaken aspects of Soteriades's study regarding Callium. Soteriades's greatest mistake was that he excluded Evrytania from any research by "stating that Karpenisi is completely missing in ancient times, and there is not any trace of a city existing there even of small significance."[71] He considered it a waste of time for the "wise" and "bureaucratic" to be occupied researching in Evrytania, claiming that the state of Evrytania was without any significant ancient history, without any contribution to our historical evolution, and without a significant contribution in the struggle for independence in 1821. Therefore, Soteriades's conclusion was that it did not offer any benefit to occupy oneself with Evrytania.

Even though Soteriades accepts that Pausanias writes with "perfect historical precision," Soteriades is nevertheless still prejudiced against Evrytania. Wrongly influenced by William Woodhouse, Soteriades does not follow the writings of Pausanias. For that reason, the readers of Soteriades's study will be falsely informed that Callium is located in Velouchovo of Doris. However, a consequence of this misunderstanding is that Soteriades's readers will not be able to understand which road was followed by the Galatians to get to Velouchovo. Soteriades speculates to a certain extent, and then he stops and starts another hypothesis. And one hypothesis refutes the other. In the end, none of the hypotheses he makes satisfy him. That is because he does not have any historical findings in Velouchovo to evidence this, as there were no archaeological findings there. Let us set forth a few passages from Soteriades's incorrect study that clearly point to his contradictions:

> a) "The disaster that the Galatians suffered is described by Pausanias with perfect historical precision and to Pausanias we must attribute the claim of valuable writer who transmitted to us credible historical sources, which otherwise would have been completely unknown events."[72]

And further on Soteriades writes:

> But, I wonder, what road did the Galatians take back, которая ended with disaster awaiting them? Pausanias says, *"ekomizonto ten aftin,"* obviously this phrase has a very general meaning, but it simply means to say that the Galatians returned to the same location but not by the same exact road.[73]

We see that Soteriades first states that Pausanias writes with "perfect historical precision," and later states that, "it could have been described in a general way, meaning the return of the Galatians to the same place." This alteration from "perfect historical precision," to the general, gives Soteriades the opportunity with different presuppositions to alter (incorrectly) the name of the entire region for the road-march that the Galatians followed toward Callium.

b) Soteriades goes on to say: "Clearly, Pausanias states that, passing behind the River Spercheios and again by Thessaly, the Galatians marched and entered into Aetolia."[74]

This is immediately followed on the next page by the following: "Since the Galatians found themselves by the bridge of Spercheios and then later went to Ftiotida." Given that Pausanias states with "perfect historical precision" that the Galatians were on their way to Aetolia, which he himself admits, why does he change the road to say Ftiotida?

c) And then, on page 308 of his book, Soteriades writes, "The Galatian Army Corps must have threatened the Aetolians within their own land. But if Callium were located near Oita at the boundaries of Aetolia, there was no danger at all for the Aetolians." And on page 311 of his book Soteriades writes, "Thus, according to the text, Callium must be sought toward the north at the edge of Korakos in Oita."

In the first case, Soteriades exhorts us to exclude that Callium was located in Oita at the boundaries of Aetolia. In the second case, he exhorts us to seek the location of Callium "around Oita." Which should we do? At this point it is obvious that Soteriades is confused since he lost the historical course that Pausanias mentions to the city of Callium. In this, Woodhouse misled Soteriades. And this becomes obvious from a statement, "Woodhouse identified Callium with the castle of Kastriotissas. This was also the idea of the first archaeologists of Greece who studied the area of Kastriotissas, which was named the city of Callium, presupposing that Callium was located here."[75]

Thus, Soteriades concludes that Callium must be sought around Oita. However, what are the elements that point to such a claim that Callium was located around Oita, since Pausanias is pushed aside? Pausanias was the only one who preserved the events of that time, otherwise they would have been absolutely unknown. It does not make sense that Callium would be located in Oita, if Callium, which was the city of Aetolia that was destroyed by the Galatians, would not have been in any danger at all if it were in Oita.

According to Soteriades, "All of these difficulties are removed, and we all agree, according to our presuppositions that the only possible march of the Galatians where Callium is sought is the castle of Velouchovo."[76] However, because Soteriades's position is based on Woodhouse's underlying wrong presuppositions, the conclusion of this author regarding these contradictory points is that Callium was not located in Oita, but in Evrytania, the main reason being that there was no danger in Oita for the Aetolians from the Galatians.

Mistaken Acceptance of Soteriades's Position
Despite the contradictory positions of Soter-

iades, ultimately and unfortunately there was, in this author's opinion, mistaken approval of the location of ancient Callium at Velouchovo, as most contemporary historians accepted the groundless position of Mr. Soteriades. One of the first to accept this position was Nicholas Polites, who in 1915, as president of the local council of "changing the names of settlements and communities," relied on Soteriades who was able in 1907 to fix the location of the ancient city of Callium in the Castle of Velouchovo."[77]

As Polites mentions in his thoughts on changing the names, he changed the names from Velouchovo to Callium or Kallipolis. For more detailed information on this great issue see Fallis's book, *Kallion Evrytanias*, pp. 78-84. Thus, the way was opened for all historians to write regarding the Galatians and Callium based only on the probability stated by Soteriades. And most importantly, many historians who until then had believed that Callium was in Evrytania, in Klapsi, changed their view. Thus, they teach:

a) Papatheodorou: "Callium was not located in Evrytania as was previously believed, but in Phocida around Velouchovo that was named Callium."[78]

b) Panos Vasileiou: "We cannot exclude Klapsi of Evrytania, which was destroyed by the Galatians, however this was not the ancient Callium."[79]

c) Nicholas Papachatzes: "Up to 1907, when the study of G. Soteriades appeared, the invi-

Callium 73

tation of the Galatians in Aetolia and the city of Callium, all believed that Callium was located in Evrytania. Now, however, not so. Now all believe that Callium was in Velouchovo."[80]

What is paradoxical, however, is that even today both Greek and non-Greek historians and archaeologists do not have any archaeological findings that prove that Callium was in Velouchovo, Doris. Historical proof is not existent. They saw the location of ancient Callium ONLY with the eyes of Soteriades, and the contradictory and unproven presentation of Soteriades's study.

For example, Gerasimos Katopodes, in his book, *Aetolian Commonwealth*, published in 1977, writes, "For the Galatian invasion of Aetolia, we follow faithfully G. Soteriades."[81] It is inconceivable to us that, even though archaeologists have found nothing that proves, with even a remote possibility, that the city of Callium was in Velouchouvo, we are shocked when they write, "The identification of ancient Callium is confirmed by irrefutable proof."[82] But the irrefutable proof is "mainly" the incorrect research of Soteriades. We would like to mention the doctoral dissertation, *The Stamps of the Aetolians Kallipolis*, which states, "Kallipolis (Callium)... was identified with the Castle of Velouchovo, mainly based on the topographical research of G. Soteriades."[83]

Callium, the Capital City

According to our research on Callium, our findings point to Evrytania as the location of Callium. There is more evidence that the city of Callium was located in Evrytania, in present-day Klapsi (also known as Klafsi).

Thus, some may ask why I make such an insistence to indicate the precise location of Callium in Evrytania, and why I persist to reverse the accepted but mistaken historical belief. The reasons for my persistence are many, and it is not possible to make a full exposition here. But one key reason is that we consider it unacceptable and harmful to our national history for historians to lay a historical edifice on an incorrect foundation. And naturally under these conditions, we will never be able to acquire an integrated national conscience and identity of our being without the correct knowledge of our history. There are cities that experienced such shocking events that forever crippled and changed the life and the course of our nation. They were places of sacrifices and holocausts for our freedom and redemption. It is unacceptable for these cities to be buried without knowing the events that happened there. But it is even more unacceptable to change the name and location of a city, and thus to lose sight of the causes and seriousness of their great contributions toward national "becoming."

Such a city was Callium, which possessed a

rich ancient history and a majesty that set the foundation for the existence of the Greek nation today. According to the rudimentary information we have found, and from what we have been able to conjecture, the city of Callium was a great city in Evrytania. It was the capital of Evrytania and more generally an important city of the Aetolian Commonwealth. The city of Callium experienced events that helped form the Greek nation. One may even say that the city of Callium in Evrytania experienced events that became resplendent lighthouses for the entire world. With great interest, at this point we will pursue what Callium was, and with even more precision, we shall write further to set the foundation of Callium's historical location.

Position of Some Historians

W. Smith in his book, *Geographic Dictionary*, writes, "The location of the Callians is defined by the location of its capital city Callium. And the position of the latter is fixed by that of their capital town Callium."[84] And a little further down, W. Smith states, "Callium or Kallipolis: the chief town of the Callians." As we especially see here, the second position is stated by W. Smith, who writes, "the chief town," that is the capital city of the Callians. Also, William Woodhouse places Callium or Kallipolis near the Maurolithari, in Kastriotissa of Doris. Woodhouse writes, "This must be Callium or Kallipolis, the chief town of the Callians," that is the capital city of the Kallieis.⁸⁵

K.D. Stergiopoulos in his book, *Ancient Aetolia*, writes: "In the confluence of the rivers Dafnous and Kokkinopotamou, in the eastern foot of the mountain, is the ancient Callium or Kallipolis, the famous capital city of the Callians, which the residents of that region called at that time."⁸⁶ With the same certainty that other historians also write that Callium was the capital city of the Callians, I will finish with the statement of the Evrytanian historian P.I. Vasileiou, despite the fact that he also could not avoid the erroneous position of the other historians that Callium was located in Doris. Vasileiou did conclude that there was a possibility "that the capital city of Evrytania was located in present-day Klapsi under another name."⁸⁷

Historically, therefore, this laid the foundation that in fact Callium was the capital of the Callians and the Evrytanian region and the Aetolian Commonwealth. Evrytania at that time "constituted the largest area of the Aetolians" (Thucydides III 94), both in population and in area. It is significant that Pausanias agrees with this position (X, 16, 4) that Evrydamos, the general of the Aetolian military at Thermopylae and then at Kokkalia who destroyed the Galatians, was from Callium. This position is confirmed by Gerasimos Katopodes, who writes: "Thus, we have Aetolian leadership of the highest class that came from Callium..."[88]

In the next chapter, you will read about how the Galatians strategically chose to destroy the city of Callium, and only Callium, suddenly and completely. The Galatians made this decision to attack Callium because it was the heart of the Aetolians, their capital and home city. This confirms our point that the city of Callium was located in Evrytania (Aetolia).

The Local Tradition Regarding Callium

For a deeper, more firmly established foundation of history, every historian must research and uncover every possible source from which they are able to draw information. Such a source with broad and deep roots lays in tradition. Local tradition is not a fossil of the past but a living function of today whose purpose it is to help us construct tomorrow. Because "tradition," according to Michael Dufrenne, "is not only a social event objectified in the institutions of customs into which we submit. It is the inner presence of our past that makes us sensitive to the influence of the social events."[89] We should compare our ancestral traditions to an invisible thread that reaches back to the time of the events without the intermediate ages cutting into it. Only time has weakened the traditions' memory and discolored their splendor, adding or subtracting elements that caused damage. For this reason, much care is needed in research to scrub the traditions properly in order to reach the "seed" of the event that remained intact. And that is why, if we lack sufficient, clear written text or found subjects, our last resort is tradition. And this tradition is that unwritten history, which is only written in the hearts and the memories of that people, and handed down like the heritage from father to children. There is a rich tradition that is known throughout the area of Klapsi that "here in Klapsi was located the ancient city of Callium that the barbarians destroyed." Perhaps there is no other area of our country of Greece where there is not such a strong and living tradition as in Klapsi. The people there retain the horror at the complete destruction of the ancient city of Callium that the Galatians imposed on it. For certain, that is a memory that has remained vivid in Klapsi over the millennia. Our fathers held the thread of the tragic events of the past, and kept it tightly tied to the events themselves, back to our roots of the past and back to the destruction of Callium. In the book, *Kallion Evrytanias*, the author Demetrios Fallis, makes mention of a dialogue between two very old men at Klapsi, that of Lefteris Gioldasis and Nikos Demetriou, where they talked about the devastation in Klapsi during the Second World War. Gioldasis stated, "This is our fate." Nikos Demetriou said, "That does not leave us green trees. From the time of the Galatians, we are left with an unhealed wound until today, we always have wars." "Nikos, you are right," answered Gioldasis in a coarse voice. "We suffered very much later. The Turks reduced us to 'weeping.'" [*Translator's Note: "Klapsi" is the modern Greek word for weeping or crying.*]

This is the living tradition of Klapsi. This tradition tied Klapsi to the ancient city of Callium, and was accepted by all historians on the location of Callium until 1907. Even historian N.G. Polites accepted this position in his book, *Paradoseis* (Athens, 1904), that the location of ancient Callium was in Klapsi (that is, before the circulation of Soteriades's book in 1907, which stated that the location of Callium was in Velouchovo). N.G. Polites writes, "In the municipality of Karpenisi in Evrytania, the villages of Laspi and Klapsi were within the municipality of Karpenisi, and for Klapsi, the weeping… the historical event of the invasion and massacre by the Galatians in 279 BC is even mentioned in the local traditions of Klapsi."[90]

Findings of Ancient Objects in Klapsi

Despite the fact that there has not been an archaeological excavation in Klapsi, and Evrytania in general, to prove with the finding of ancient artifacts that the ancient city of Callium was located in Evrytania, there have surfaced various broken, but useful, objects that confirm that Klapsi was the location of ancient Callium. This includes "…foundations of structures, mosaics on the floor, tombs, coins, ceramic handicrafts, and other objects..." that confirm the existence of an ancient city and a great civilization. These findings were found on the surface as well as two and a half meters deep. In unofficial excavations that some people made in the area of Agioi Taxiarchae a few years ago, the people uncovered a portico that tradition had said was there; there came to light many foundations of buildings and thousands of crushed roof tiles.[91] We now have a finding of objects that have surfaced, dated to the end of the fifth century BC and after. The finding of these objects confirms that there was a flourishing civilization, and that Callium was the capital, and this was certainly not manufactured this century. These objects confirm that there is a significant gap in history that is lost from the time of Homer and even earlier from the time of Evrytos and Oechalia!

Agios Leonides

As we said earlier, our Evrytanian ancestors were pious people and that helped them develop a greater society that led to a good quality of life. The irrefutable affirmation of this is the church of Agios (Saint) Leonides in Klapsi. This church, as the inscriptions reveal, was built during the Byzantine period in the fifth century AD and is the most closely associated with Saint Leonides. The reason we make reference to this fifth century Christian church here is because its history and its people go back to the time of ancient Evrytania before Christ. In the author's book, *Kallion Evrytanias*, pp. 38-40 and pp. 107-124, we analyzed this church at length, however here we confine ourselves to presenting only the findings of objects relating to the centuries before Christ. Certainly, today the church of Agios Leonides, known as the Basilica of Klapsi, is the most significant historical monument, both in Evrytania but also generally in western Greece, since there have not been excavations elsewhere to find another monument to prove to the contrary. The inscriptions in this church, though completed in the fifth century AD, bear witness to the civilization that existed there before Christ.

Translator's Note: We take a moment to bring attention to Agios Leonides and his seven female disciples. Agios Leonides and his seven female disciples were missionaries in Central Greece—Evrytania in the third century AD. They brought Christianity to the people of central Greece. Agios Leonides was the choir director of this group of seven female disciples. The number seven is important, as the early Christians praised God in choirs of seven people.

Agios Leonides, accompanied by the seven female disciples suffered martyrdom in Corinth in 258 AD. According to the Patmian Code, they were captured by the authorities during Divine Liturgy on Holy Saturday and thrown into the Corinthian Gulf. They did not drown, but instead, they rose up and walked on the water, as if on land, singing hymns. They were then recaptured. Their captors tied stones around their necks and drowned them.

In the church of Agios Leonides, it is interesting to note that on the left of the ciborium (a holy vessel) an inscription has survived: "Polygeros the devoted reader and Andromache the God-Loving [Deaconess] are asking for the prayers of Agios Leonides and the seven disciples." In the rest of the space of the holy sanctuary there are small designs and many and various images such as birds and fishes. Besides the holy table, there is a spacious area that includes the synthrono—the bishop's throne, even though we do not know any details of a bishop's throne or a bishop's presence in Evrytania at that time. It is of interest to byzantinists to study this church's architecture. For more information and a description of the church, see the excellent book by the same author, Demetrios Fallis, Agios Leonides, His Martyrs, His Identity, The Ancient Church in Klapsi *(Klauseion)*, Athens (1999), pp. 158-168.

Apolytikion hymn of Agios Leonides (in the Third Tone):

> A great champion, you are called, in Epidauros, O Leonides, you were not daunted by the hindrance of Beliar; having destroyed the worship of the idols and bravely confessing Christ, with the seven women O all-blessed one, fervently entreat on our behalf that we may be given great mercy.

This is confirmed by the inscription we found in the Central Square of the sanctuary (6.83 x

5.70 m.) from marble bases taken from the previous building that existed there. From the marble bases the inscription was cut and fastened on the trunk of the Kolyma box, and after covering them they were embroidered on the floor in the inscription in the center, before the place where the holy altar was located (1.39 x 1.70 m) in thirteen lines that were sufficiently preserved from the length of time. The inscription reads:

> During the time of Eutychion and Polycarpou, the Right Reverend presbyters and Melisou the Right Reverend Reader and Economos of this Holy Church and all the God-loving Clergy, this temple was rebuilt in honor of the all-glorious Saint Leonides, and the embroidering on the floor was made.[92]

The term ἀνεκαινίσθη or "rebuilt" in the tenth line of the inscription can only be interpreted to mean that there preexisted a temple, perhaps a smaller one. In 490 AD when it was rebuilt, the inscription was made in the form, which was found during the excavations of 1957. It is certain that the present structure was built on a preexisting and perhaps a pagan temple because there are "four marble bases, remnants from earlier structure" as we mentioned before.

The Basilica of Klapsi reveals to us other facts that we have mentioned in the book, *Kallion Evrytanias*, and we will not repeat them here. It would, however, be an omission if we did not mention here an identical text appearing there. Emanuel Hatzedakes writes,

It is noteworthy that the only formed piece of marble was a piece of the base of copper of a statue used as a crown. There was no stone whatsoever, only an architectural piece that indicated poor condition, but the movable pieces were very sparse: small lamps, iron nails, a blade of small knife, etc. We noticed especially that outside the wall of the main arch of the sanctuary three small piles of shattered window glass, chestnut sheet indicating the corresponding place of the true windows of the sanctuary. (Emanuel Hatzedakes, ΠΑΕ 1958, excavation of the Basilica of Klapsi, p. 61).

Regarding the excavation of the holy temple of Agios Leonides, Mr. Hatzedakes writes that the objects that were found "were very sparse." Nevertheless, in actuality, the people from Klapsi who were present at the excavation[93] found that the objects were not "very sparse" but that there were many more. Unfortunately, however, we do not know where the other objects are. We do not know if they have been neglected or lost. We hope they have not been lost to history. This would be very sad indeed.

Let us summarize the information that we have stated regarding the church of Agios Leonides, which is that we may conclude that in this Byzantine Christian monument, the ancient world met with renewed spirit the history of Callium in Klapsi, and created a remarkable civilization in Evrytania. Even though this church was not the first or only church in Callium at that time, it was the largest. That is evident from the measurements of the church: (28 m x 18½ m) (91.86 ft x 60.7 ft) and (518m^2) (5,576 sf). It was the cathedral where the bishop presided, in particular a Bishop Aemilianos, as well as the many other clergy who served in this church: three priests, two readers, one deaconess, one subdeacon, and one deacon. These numbers of clergy indicate the spirit of the high intellectual level of Evrytania. There were also precious inscriptions in the artistic embroiderings on the ground. And this was at a time when Christianity was at its beginning and there were difficult times, and also the church was in a mountainous place and inaccessible. All these elements point to the fact with certainty that there flourished in Evrytania a large Christian community with a high intellectual and cultural level.[94]

Historical Proof

Up to now, we have relied on local tradition and the finding of shattered pre-Christian objects in the location of Klapsi to prove that Callium was located at Klapsi of Evrytania and not at Velouchovo of Doris. However, although the shattered objects certainly give evidence of the ancient existence of the village, they say nothing about its name, Callium. If we connect the rich traditions of the village, they fit perfectly with the name Callium. And were it not for the historical mistake of Soteriades in 1907, and the change of the name Velouchovo in a different region (the region of Doris) to Callium by Nicholas G. Polites (1915), then there would not have been any problem for the name since Klapsi until 1961 had in its possession the seal of their community, the name "Callium."

We believe that the location of the city of Callium in Evrytania can be proven historically. We are convinced that, even if the shattered findings and the tradition were missing from Klapsi, the ancient historians such as Thucydides and Pausanias would still lead us to the fact that Callium had not been located in Doris, and instead would direct us to the location of Callium in Evrytania. The positions of these ancient historians are numerous, and for this reason we will make a selection of the two most important positions that support our own views for the location of Callium in Evrytania, that of Thucydides and Pausanias.

Thucydides

Thucydides was the most critical of historical writers and wrote only that of which he was certain with accuracy and precision. He himself writes, "The history... has been written by... Thucydides, an Athenian... who formed judgments and followed with close attention, so as to acquire accurate information."[95] Having this in mind, we must pay close attention to Thucydides and have trust in his writings. Basically,

Callium

Thucydides is the first and most important historical writer who provides us with clear information of ancient Aetolia and the Aetolians in the fifth century BC. In his book of history, Thucydides writes:

> The Aetolian Commonwealth was indeed great and polemic, they were a great warlike people, but as they lived in unwalled villages, which, however, were widely separated, and as used only in light armor, they could be subdued without difficulty before they could unite for mutual defense... The Evrytanians, the largest division of the Aetolians, their speech is more unintelligible than the other Aetolians, and according to report, they are eaters of raw flesh. If these tribes were subdued they said, the rest would readily yield. They marched toward Aetolia. On the first day they took Potidanian, on the second day Krokylei, on the third day Teichion. There they remained, sending their booty back to Eupalium in Locris... But all the preparations did not escape the notice of the Aetolians, neither when the designs were first formed nor afterwards; indeed his army had no sooner invaded their country than they all began to rally in the great forest, so that help came even from the remotest tribes of the Ophioneans, who stretched as far as Malian Gulf, and from the Bomians and Callians. (Thucydides III 94, 95)

Let us stop here for a moment and critically study the small text of Thucydides. Let us pay attention to some of his points that Callium was removed completely from Velouchovo. The certainty is that the Aetolian nations consisted of the Apodotians, Ophioneans, and after them the Evrytanians. That the Evrytanians consisted of the largest part of the Aetolians means that they possessed the largest territorial land and the largest population. Thus, it is obvious that since the Evrytanians were the largest tribe, it logically follows that the capital city was located in Evrytania. This is clarified by Thucydides himself when he makes the point that, on the first, second, and third days, Demosthenes captured the three cities: Potidania, Krokyleio, and Teichio. All these cities were outside of Aetolia. As Thucydides says, "And when the Army of Demosthenes invaded their country of Aetolia, then they all began to rally in great force." Therefore, Velouchovo was not part of the Aetolian territory. Of this fact we are convinced, because when the Galatians advanced, "All began to rally in great force, so that help came even from the most remote nations of the Ophioneans, who stretched as far as the Malic Gulf, and from the Bomians *and Callians (emphasis added)*." The battlefield for this battle was in the region of Doris, where Velouchovo is located. How then were the Callians considered "the most remote" if Callium were right there in Velouchovo? So, Thucydides gives firm witness that Callium was not in Velouchovo, but in the territory of Evrytania.

Pausanias

Pausanias is even clearer in his certainty that the city of Callium was in Evrytania. The description he gives is very familiar, and we can see he is the historian of Callium. In analyzing and interpreting Pausanias, we could write a whole book about the march of the Galatians and the destruction of Callium. The destruction is extremely shocking, and Pausanias includes many details of events. We gather from Pausanias two positions that demonstrate with certainty the march of the Galatians from Thermopylae to Callium in Evrytania, and the Galatians' return the same way.

In the summer of 279 BC, about 213,000 Galatian army troops, led by Brennus, their commander, descended from Macedonia with their goal to invade Delphi and to loot the riches there. They passed through Thessaly and continued, crossed the bridge of the Spercheios River to eventually reach Thermopylae. At Thermopylae, the united Greek army repelled the Galatians. Thus, the Galatians had no hope of reaching their goal, Delphi. Then the Galatian commander, Brennus, for diversion detached about 40,000 soldiers from his numerous army foot soldiers and 800 cavalry to attack Aetolia. Thus, Pausanias writes, "But Brennus reasoned that if he could compel the Aetolians to return home to Aetolia [to defend their people and their land], he would find the war against

Greece prove easier thereafter. So he detached from his army 40,000 foot soldiers and about 800 horse[men to go to Aetolia]. Over these he set in command Orestorius and Combutis, who, making their way back by way of the bridges over the Spercheios [River] and across Thessaly again, invaded Aetolia."[96]

Let us briefly analyze, geographically, the position that Pausanias sets forth regarding the invasion of Aetolia by the Galatians that was "through Thessaly." We ask simply of those who insist that Callium was located in Doris, how was it possible geographically for the Galatians to have crossed "the Bridges of the River Spercheios backwards," to reach Thessaly, and come to Doris to destroy Velouchovo, which they say at that time was Callium? Velouchovo of Doris was to the south of Thessaly. Whatever side we examine, we find it impossible! However, we know that Klapsi is within what was then Aetolia, and that the Galatians invaded through Thessaly. We know that the Galatians marched to Evrytania through Thessaly and then also returned to Thermopylae by the same way, and not through the south, by Velouchovo of Doris. Pausanias writes: "When the barbarians [the Galatians], having pillaged houses and structures and having set on fire Callium, returning by the same way." [*Translator's Note: These additional citations are included here in brackets: Pausanias, X, 22, Papyros Publications, Trans. A.*

Papatheodorou; Pausanias, *Description of Greece*, The Loeb Classical Library (Harvard University Press, Cambridge, MA, 1979), Trans. W.H.S. Jones, IV, Book VIII (22) – X, p. 495.]

It is obvious from the foregoing statement by Pausanias that the Galatians, after they invaded and completely destroyed Callium in Evrytania, began to return to Thermopylae by the same road that they had gone to Callium. We ask again: How can it be possible, geographically, for the Galatians to return to Thermopylae by the same road, if Callium had been in Velouchovo of Doris, which was south of Thessaly? See below for more details on this topic in the related section on the Battle of Kokkalia.

Let us summarize the positions of the ancient historians, both Thucydides and Pausanias. It is obvious that both historians exclude the location of Callium from Doris and lead their steps with certainty to Evrytania. We would like to complete this brief reference to Callium with the works of Michael Staphyla, who remarks, "With numerous objects and methods, Fallis proves and manages to refute many views that place Callium outside of Evrytania. On the basis of the written witnesses of the ancient historians, the later findings, the rich tradition of Klapsi, it is clear that ancient Callium is the present-day Klapsi. Fallis worked very hard, and toiled as he researched in his perfect studies and refuted the contrary positions."[97]

Finally, we quote from the *Encyclopedia Papyros* the refutation of the view that Callium was located in Velouchovo of Doris, "From the noteworthy events we mentioned the defense against the Galatians in 279 BC, which was of the Kokkalia Krikellou-Laspis of Evrytania, where the Galatians suffered terrible losses and that only a small group survived due to the fact that it was covered by the thick forest and thus reached Thessaly. Since that time, due to the fact that in this region numerous bones were found in this place, for this reason this region is named Kokkalia."[98] [*Translator's Note: the significance of the name Kokkalia will be explained in the next chapter.*]

The aforementioned positions reinforce without question that Callium was in Evrytania.

IV. KOKKALIA

Translator's Note: In this chapter, the author describes the battles of Callium (located in present-day Klapsi in Evrytania as explained in the previous chapter) and Kokkalia (the present-day name for a subsequent battleground in Evrytania) in 279 BC. They were existential battles to save the Evrytanians as well as the entire Greek nation.

Forgotten Evrytanian Glory

It is imperative that we state here without ambivalence the fact that the ancient Evrytanians made a foundational contribution to the struggles for our establishment as a Greek nation. Without a doubt, Evrytanians have an ancient and glorious history. The Evrytanians contributed much, and gave it all, in the critical moments of our national welfare and kept nothing for themselves. However, they lost, with the passage of time, not only their belongings but even their own glorious history. So much historical information regarding their sacrifices remains unknown to the world but also to the Evrytanians. Shocking struggles that laid the foundations of national integrity and indescribable sacrifices that watered the tree of our people for numerous millennia, these remain completely unknown to us. Today we can speak historically, and responsibly, in spite of the still insufficient research, of the great struggles we made for freedom during the fifth century before Christ. Heroes of the "first" magnitude in Thermopylae struggling for a national existence. National martyrs—men, women, and children—complete holocausts—in Callium. Unrepeatable in heroic self-sacrifice of women at Kokkalia in the third century BC and saints and martyrs of our faith during the Roman period. However, all these are buried (in the dirt or in the libraries) and are unknown to us. All these thousands of heroes and martyrs are our ancestors who created these great historical pinnacles of our national survival we enjoy today as Greeks, as Orthodox, and as free people.

Therefore, we must research, to conduct excavation without any delay—in the entire area of Evrytania—to bring to the surface all the ancient buried "villages" and "cities"[99] in order for us to know our history and its real dimension. Because presently our national education does not mention one of the greatest events of Greek history:

- the invasion of the Galatians in southern Greece in 279 BC
- the Aetolian conflict with the Galatians in Thermopylae
- the radical destruction of Callium and the

massacre and holocaust of the Callians
- the survival of Greece by the crushing of the Galatians by the Evrytanians at the battleground in present-day Kokkalia.

The Invasion of the Galatians

The Galatians basically were a people that did not have a specific nation. Many historians consider the Galatians a tribe. Other historians, the majority, identify the Galatians (also called Gauls in English), with the Celts. Perhaps the Galatians were the most important of all the Celtic tribes. Much points to the position that the Galatians and the Celts were one people. It was the group of people who spoke the Indo-European language and first appeared in the second millennium BC in Central Europe between Germany and France, what is today Switzerland, with the name Celts. "The study of toponomy defines in the southeast of Germany a triangle between the Rhine and the Danube that represents, without a doubt, the original settlement of the Celts."[100]

The historian Pausanias, a traveler, insists that the Celts later were named and were known as Galatians. In his *Phocis* (Ch. 3 and 19-23), Pausanias names these barbarians who invaded the Greek soil with their leader Brennus in the third century BC. Sometimes they were called Celts or Galatians. [Pausanias, *Description of Greece*, The Loeb Classical Library (Harvard University Press, Cambridge, MA, 1979), Trans. W.H.S. Jones, Book I, IV, p. 19.]

Pausanias goes on to say that the Galatians mobilized their army to invade Greece beyond the boundaries of the country—their first foreign expedition was under the leadership of Cambaules. [Pausanias, *Description of Greece*, The Loeb Classical Library (Harvard University Press, Cambridge, MA, 1979), Trans. W.H.S. Jones, IV, Books VIII (22) – X, pp. 473-475.] Today, the well-known statue of a "Galatian dying" is in the Capitoline Museum in Rome and wears a Celtic braided necklace as an identification of the Celtic tribe. This points to the fact that these people were the same people. These Galatians preserved their Celtic customs and language during the Roman period in the time when Saint Jerome (348-420 AD) visited their land, and they still spoke the Celtic language.[101] The Celtic language was spoken in the Middle Ages throughout western Europe in the present-day British Isles, France, Lombardy, the Iberian Peninsula, Slovenia, Croatia, Hungary, and in a great area of the Peninsula of Aemon and in the Asia Minor Galatian.[102]

Over time the Galatians succeeded to penetrate into most of the European nations without, however, being able to create their own nation. The time of their great spread was the first millennium BC. In the sixth century BC, they settled in the Iberian Peninsula. Then in the fifth and fourth centuries BC, they descended into Italy and Massilia (present-day Marseilles, France). Finally, in the third century BC, the Galatians invaded Macedonia, Thessaly, and the mainland of Greece.

> Thus, the Celtic expansion reached the most distant points in the third century, the boundaries of the Celtic adventure are defined by the names they occupied such as Galatia, Galicia, etc. However, the Celtic tribes were unable to attain the conception of a nation. The Celts never made an effort to create an empire. They held onto the conquered lands and on the contrary the dispersion weakened their weak association of independent tribes.[103]

Regarding the Galatian invasion of Macedonia and later of mainland Greece, I.G. Papastavrou writes,

> Brennus invaded Macedonia by the so-called iron gates (*Demi Kapou*). He was opposed by Sosthenes and did not allow him to settle there, after much struggle that was not decisive. Brennus in the fall of 279 marched to the mainland of Greece that recently won its independence.[104]

The history of the Galatian invasion of Greek soil has been preserved with numerous details by the ancient historian Pausanias. Soteriades [cited earlier] writes that Pausanias is the only one from the ancient historians "with trustworthy sources who writes historical facts and preserved for us what otherwise would have been completely unknown events to us."[105]

Therefore, we will convey from Pausanias's book, *Phocis*, some relevant extracts related to the Galatians' invasion of the Aetolian Callium, the crimes they committed, and finally their break up by the lion-hearted Evrytanian women in Kokkalia, "who were full of wrath against the Galatians."

The story begins in Thermopylae, where the Greek and Galatian armies met. The fierce army of the Galatians in Thermopylae was great in numbers: about 152,000 foot soldiers and 20,400 in the calvary. In reality, however, the calvary had 61,200, because beside each horseman there were two servants who were good horsemen, and they also had horses. Therefore, in total with the 152,000 foot soldiers and the 61,200 calvary, the Galatian army in Thermopylae was approximately 213,200. With this kind of concentration, Brennus led the Galatians in their march against Greece.

When the Greeks saw what they were up against, they almost lost their courage, but their strong fear compelled them by necessity to defend Greece. They saw that the impending struggle was not to retain their freedom, as in their wars against the Medes, but to fight to save themselves from extinction. The Greeks realized that they would not be saved from the Galatians, even if they had offered earth and water, a sign of surrender. They fought to save themselves from the same suffering that the

Macedonians, the Thracians, and the Paiones suffered during their invasion by the Galatians. The contemporary Galatian crimes against the Thessalians became infamous. Every citizen, and every city therefore, must be victorious or be wiped off of the earth! In order to defend their country against the barbaric Galatians, the Greeks concentrated in Thermopylae as follows: 2,000 armed soldiers and 500 horsemen from Boeotia, with their leaders Kephisodotos, Thearidas, Diogenes, and Lysandros. From the Phoceis, 500 horsemen and 3,000 foot soldiers were under the command of generals Critoboulos and Antiochos. The commanders from the island of Atalantes Locrous were under Meidias: there were 700 foot soldiers, but they did not have any cavalry. From Megara there were 400 foot soldiers and their commander was from the Megara Kipponikos. The Aetolian army was a large number and suitable for every kind of battle, however, they did not mention the number of the cavalry. However, it is believed that the total cavalry was 790, and more than 7,000 foot soldiers of the Aetolians were under Polyarchos, Polyphron, and Lakrates. The Athenian commander was Callipos of Moirocleous. Their power was all suitable for sailing boats, 500 horsemen and 1,000 foot soldiers. Due to their former glory, the Athenians had the general leadership.

When Brennus marched into Heracleian, he

was informed by the Greek deserters that it was a big Greek army and from where they came to Thermopylae. The next day the battle began at sunrise. The Galatians proceeded forward against the Greeks in a frenzied, irrational attack, like manic beasts. The Galatians disregarded even when the Greeks were hit, and continued to dismember them with axes or knives. However, the Greeks were fierce as well, and as long as they breathed, they would fight fiercely. The leaders therefore of the barbaric Galatians terrorized the Greeks who became perplexed about the future, seeing that the present understanding was not going well at all.

Realizing that the Aetolians were the strongest contingent in the Greek army, Brennus strategized that if he would force the Aetolians to return home to Aetolia, then it would be easier to fight the rest of the Greeks. He sent a detachment of 40,000 foot soldiers and 800 cavalry with Oresterios and Combutis as leaders to Aetolia by the bridge of Spercheios. They marched through Thessaly and invaded Aetolia. Oresterios and Combutis committed the greatest atrocities from all that we know and have heard, and do not resemble at all even other bold crimes against humanity. The Galatians slaughtered all human males without discrimination—including old men and infants taken from the breasts of their mothers. Of the infants that were taken from their mothers' milk, the Galatians killed them and drank their food and ate the meat! The women, especially those virgins who were preparing for marriage, those having pride, hastened to commit suicide during that time the city was conquered. The women whom the Galatians captured alive were raped. Some of the women took the knife from the Galatians, and they took their own lives. Other women gave themselves up to death because the barbarians constantly acted indecently toward them, one after the other, and even abused the dead ones. When they arrived at Callium, the Galatians plundered the houses and the holding places and burned the city of Callium to the ground.

The Aetolians in Thermopylae were informed by messengers of the calamity. As intended by Brennus, immediately and as fast as they could, the Aetolians left Thermopylae and marched to Aetolia with great indignation regarding the calamities of their people and with determination to save those cities the Galatians had not yet invaded. All the Aetolian men who were in the area, regardless of age, joined their army to overthrow the Galatians. The Aetolians fought bravely. Of the 40,800 Galatian infantry and horsemen who marched to Aetolia, fewer than half later returned alive to Thermopylae.[106] This second battle will be further described below.

The Greeks Completely Lost Their Confidence

We offer here in this small study some passages from the texts of Pausanias, which will assist us to ground our position that present-day Kokkalia is the greatest historical shrine of our nation, but at the same time is the most forgotten place by all of us. Kokkalia was the location of a large battle against the Galatians and where the Galatians were vanquished and repelled by the Aetolians. Certainly, in this author's book, *Kallion Evrytanias*, there are more than forty pages on Kokkalia. Numerous lectures have been given and numerous articles have been published in Evrytanian periodicals and newspapers on the subject of Kokkalia. But here we must briefly see certain other sides of our proofs in the new elements that we possess. And if in the future I can compile all my research to be published in one single volume, I would do so in honor of the unrepeatable contribution of this place, Kokkalia, to the Greek nation.

Here now, we emphasize in this text some phrases of Pausanias, which will constitute the epicenter of the historicity of events. And primarily we begin with the title, "The Greeks Lost Their Confidence," in combination with the rest of the phrase. In the first reading of this phrase, one may think that Pausanias exaggerates. If one carefully pays attention to the text and combines it with the remaining text, then one will confirm that Pausanias describes the events with great care, and with the necessary objectivity and historical responsibility of a respected historian.

The fact is that a great number of the barbaric Galatian army descended from Macedonia to invade the southern Greek lands. It was inevitable that the Greeks, who had just recovered their independence, might lose confidence. It was inevitable that the Greeks would look to form a coalition, not simply to fight the enemy, not simply to secure their freedom, but determined to confront them and fight to the end, in order not to be completely vanquished. The Galatians were people that fought others, not out of an injustice done to them, nor because of the expansions of the boundaries of their country—since they did not have a particular location as their country—and not because they sought to find a wealthier country to settle. The Galatians invaded wherever there were affluent areas with public wealth in order to plunder and steal. For that reason, Pausanias writes, "It was then that Brennus, both in public meetings and also in personal talks with individual Gallic officers, strongly urged the campaign against Greece, enlarging on the weakness of Greece at the time, on the wealth of the Greek states, and on the even greater wealth in sanctuaries, including votive offerings and coined silver and gold." [*Pausanias*, X, 22, Papyros Publications, Trans. A. Papatheodorou; Pausanias, *Description of Greece*, The Loeb Classical Library Library (Harvard University Press, Cambridge, MA, 1979), Trans. W.H.S. Jones, IV, Book VIII (22) – X, pp. 475-477.]

The Galatians were people who marched and invaded to pillage and plunder. As Pausanias states, the barbarians "who had tasted of the joy of plunder and acquired a passion for robbery and plunder, that a large force of infantry and no small number of mounted men attended the muster." [*Pausanias*, X, 22, Papyros Publications, Trans. A. Papatheodorou; Pausanias, *Description of Greece*, The Loeb Classical Library Library (Harvard University Press, Cambridge, MA, 1979), Trans. W.H.S. Jones, IV, Book VIII (22) – X, p. 475.]

The worst thing for each place that the Galatians invaded was that literally every aspect of life was devastated, starting with the destruction of every human life, in the worst possible way in each case. The Galatians destroyed whole cities and peoples, leaving not a trace of their existence. The city of Xyniada near Thaumaes was destroyed completely, as was the capital city of Callium, not leaving one human life, even for witness (See Dem. Fallis, *Kallion Evrytanias*, p. 172). As was stated above, no one from the city of Callium survived, except those who served in the army at Thermopylae and the women who escaped to the mountains and reached Kokkalia. The Greeks "still remembered the fate of Macedonia, Thrace and Paeonia during the former incursion of the Gauls, and reports were coming in of enormities committed at the very time on the Thessalonians." [Pausanias, *Description of Greece,* The Loeb Classical Library (Harvard University Press, Cambridge, MA, 1979), Trans. W.H.S. Jones, IV, Books VIII (22) – X, p. 479.]

The Struggle That Lies Ahead

The information the Greeks had concerning the invasion by the Galatians of other areas and the atrocities committed against them in comparison to the confrontation of the enemy and imprisoned enemies cannot be fully conveyed. That is because nothing would save them, not even surrender: "...giving water and earth [surrendering] would not bring them safety," as Pausanias says.[107] As for the greatness of the fear of the Greeks, as we saw in Pausanias's passage, we clearly see that it was justified fear. Here Pausanias, however, gives us the reason to make certain comparisons of previous dangers, especially that of the dangers from the Persians that the Greeks faced, but which were different from the invasion of the Galatians.

It is without question that the Greek nation since its most ancient times NEVER faced such a serious threat of complete destruction as in 279 BC from the barbaric and cannibalistic Galatians. This serious threat was acknowledged by all the Greeks at the time. They attributed the victory and the survival of the Greek nation mainly to the Aetolians. The trophy belonged exclusively to the Aetolians, which under the influence of the Oracle of Delphi was undisputed for many centuries.[108] This trophy, however, was completely forgotten later, and today we are not instructed in any level in Greek schooling about this pivotal event in Greek history. We learn about all the wars conducted "for freedom," with the exception of the invasion by the Galatians in 279 BC. In fact, this must be the first and foremost instruction of our history. This war took place for the survival of our nation and the existence of the Greeks, but unfortunately the great event of Kokkalia became only "mythical stories."

The history of Greek wars for the defense of freedom starts with the Medes (Persian) Wars (490-480 BC) with Marathon, Salamina, Plataies, and Mycale. It is justified that magnificent monuments were erected and became shrines for these wars. Furthermore, we know the history that we are instructed about in our schools concerning the "Thermopylae of Leonidas" with the 300 Spartans who fell fighting Xerxes in 480 BC. A splendid monument was erected there and bears the statue of Leonidas to witness the precise historical truth for this event that took place in the narrow pass of Thermopylae. The importance of this event is not debated.

Even so, let us return to our topic. Let us return to Thermopylae in 279 BC. Today we are not instructed in schools about the invasion by the Galatians and the bravery of the Aetolians. We do not know anything about the Athenian

Callipo and his generals, the Aetolian Polyarcho, Polyphrona, and Lacrate who led the united Greek armies in the harsh narrow tight pass of Thermopylae at that era and crushed the Galatians to divert the Galatians away. This attack by the Galatians was not simply for the subjugation of our people, but it was for their complete and utter destruction. And yet not even a bust was erected to honor the Phocian Telesarchus, under whose leadership the Greeks fought valiantly. "They [the Greeks] overcame the barbarians [Galatians] in this engagement, but Telesarchus himself fell, a man devoted, if ever a man was, to the Greek cause."[109] And there is nothing in honor of the gallant Athenian combatant, Cydias. "Of the Athenians themselves the bravest was Cydias, a young man who had never before been in battle. He was killed by the Gauls, but his relatives dedicated his shield to Zeus, God of Freedom, and the inscription ran: —

> Here hang I, yearning for the still useful bloom of Cydias,
> The shield of a glorious man, an offering to Zeus.
> I was the very first through which at this battle he thrust his left arm,
> When the battle raged furiously against the Gaul.[110]

Now let us compare the extent of the danger that the Greeks faced in 279 BC from the Galatians to the danger that the Greeks faced in 490-480 BC from the Persians. We are compelled to compare these events, because the event with the Galatians in 279 BC is passed over almost in silence. The war wrought by the Galatians was real and vicious, but it is not even mentioned in most history instruction. This stands in contrast to the danger brought by the Persians in 490-480 BC, which is propounded to its full extent—and in some points may even be exaggerated:

- The Persians from what we know were a cultured people, they had a great nation, an organized nation, and an old, significant history; they were always adventurous.
- The Persian wars against other nations were to conquer others, to subjugate people and to expand their empire. "They [the Greeks] realized that the struggle that faced them would not be one for liberty, as it was when they fought the Persians..."[111]
- For the Galatians, war was for "looting and plunder," and to destroy the people they conquered. On this, Pausanias is clear, as stated previously, even "giving water and earth [surrendering] would not bring them safety."[112] The Greeks, even if they offered submission to the Galatians, would not have been saved from the greatest of danger from the Galatians in comparison to the Persians or any other enemy of the Greek country.
- The Persians as warriors could have committed war crimes, but they were not bloodthirsty and cannibalistic. In contrast, the Galatians went beyond the

unrepeatable in these centuries, committing crimes of slaughter and cannibalism: "Every male they put to the sword, and they were butchered old men equally with children at their mothers' breasts. The more plump of the suckling babes the Gauls killed, drinking their blood and eating their flesh."[113]

- We can also make the comparison of the two dangers from our enemies with the numbers in their respective armies: Herodotus, according to C. Paparegopoulos, does not mention the Persian army, and says only that this army is "...numerous and well prepared." He states regarding the Persian navy that there were more than 600 galleys, so we can safely estimate, besides the sailors and the oarsmen, that there were 30,000 to 40,000 other men transported, whereas the entire Greek power was only about 10,000, or at the most 11,000 soldiers.[114]

Therefore, the army of the Persians at Marathon was about 40,000 men, while the army of the Galatians that came to Thermopylae was more than 213,000.[115]

In addition to the great number of Galatians, Pausanias writes that it is very important that "...the Celts [Galatians] as a race are far taller than any other people." [Pausanias, *Description of Greece*, The Loeb Classical Library (Harvard University Press, Cambridge, MA, 1979), Trans. W.H.S. Jones, IV, Books VIII (22) – X, p. 485.] Others say that the Greek army that came from many cities and that was concentrated in Thermopylae to fight the Galatians was approximately 25,000.[116] In any case there was a great imbalance and a hard struggle by the Greeks at this time with the Galatians; a great difference in the danger from the Galatians and the historical responsibility that they had in comparison with the danger from the Persians. For this reason, the battle was not for freedom as it was at other times against the Medica or Persians, but every citizen in every city formed the opinion that they would either all fall or all be victorious. Victory or death. There was no other choice. Pausanias says it this way, "So every man, as well as every state, was convinced that they must either conquer or perish."[117]

The Barbarians Were Alarmed

In the war at Thermopylae in 279 BC the most numerous of the Greeks who were in the best fighting condition in the Greek army were the soldiers in the Aetolian army, the men of Evrytania.[118] This was a very important factor for the outcome of the war. Certainly, Brennus knew all this from his informers. He knew the precise number of the coalition of the Greek army that blocked the path to Thermopylae and the number of soldiers from each city, including Aetolia.

Thus, based on his numerical superiority and his boldness, at sunrise Brennus began the attack on the Greek lines. The Galatians began their attack with anger and irrational fury against the Greeks, trying to break through the lines and channel great losses to the attackers.

The attacks of the Galatians took many days, battle after battle. The barbarians were alarmed by the Greeks and were perplexed. For the first time they saw that their strategic engagements were not going well. Then, the cunning Brennus, as Pausanias says, "reasoned that if he could compel the Aetolians to return home to Aetolia, he would find the war against Greece would prove much easier. So, Brennus detached from his army 40,000 foot soldiers and about 8,000 horsemen. Over these he put in command Orestorius and Combutis, who, making their way back by way of the Bridge of Spercheios, marched across through Thessaly again, and invaded Aetolia."[119]

This passage of Pausanias was quoted earlier, and we are repeating it here again to draw close attention to the march of the Galatians toward Callium, its destruction, and the return of the Galatians by the same path where they then suffered total destruction in Kokkalia.

Orestorius and Combutis received orders from Brennus to invade Aetolia and to destroy the capital city of Callium. This order of Brennus was to be kept a secret in order to be executed quickly and to its fullness because winter was near. The Galatians passed the Bridge of Spercheios again and headed for Thessaly the same way, indicating the constant losses to the Greeks were a large part of the reason for Brennus's army to leave for Macedonia where they had begun. We can imagine the Greeks felt relief that the barbarians left for Macedonia.

The march of the Galatians to Thessaly was from the well-known way down to Thermopylae. When the Galatians arrived in Thessaly, they followed left (west) to the way of Aetolia. This naturally interprets the position of Pausanias: "They marched through Thessaly and invaded Aetolia."[120] This way through Thessaly and generally western Greece was a great central way that connected the commercial and strategic means from the ancient times with the eastern crease and reached to the Thermos and Akarnania. In this march of the Galatians until they reached Aetolia—Callium was their specific target—they faced three minor obstacles, which they found a way to overcome:

- The small city of Xyniada surprised the Galatians, which led to destroying all its residents in order not to have any survivors to give information to the Aetolians about their march toward Aetolia.[121]
- A small garrison of Aetolians who were stationed at Kokkalia, which they surprised and destroyed.

- The destruction of a small tower in the highest point in the entrance, northeast of Callium.

The continuation of their path was open for violence like frenzied monsters upon Callium.

On Their Mothers' Breasts

I mentioned above the indescribable crimes that the Greek people faced from the beasts from the north, the cannibalistic Galatians in their invasion of Callium and I will elaborate on them with more detail here. "Pausanias was a traveler. He lived through wars and saw many things. And naturally he heard about many more, which in his narration were terrible and bold, and that were unbelievable nightmarish stories. In spite of these, the crimes of the Galatians against the civilians of Callium surpassed even the boldest imaginations." For that reason, Pausanias notes that, "Although the Callians suffered so terribly that even Homer's account of Laestrygones[122] and the Cyclops does not seem outside the truth, yet they were duly and fully avenged." Again, as Pausanias states:

> The fate of the Callians at the hands of Combutis and Orestorius is the most wicked ever heard of, and is without a parallel in the crimes of men. Every male they put to the sword, and there were butchered old men equally with children at their mothers' breasts. The more plump of these suckling babes the Gauls killed, drinking their blood and eating their flesh.[123]

These were terrible and indescribable "in

cold blood' crimes to be committed by an army on civilians and an undefended population; or in any event a group that calls itself an army and not mad beasts. As is obvious from what Pausanias says, the Galatians were mad and wild beasts who ate the flesh of the "more plump" infants. This was cannibalism of the worst, wild type. What more horrible action could Pausanias about write than this? And what worse man could there be?

Is there in the human evil another step down? What else could we add to the description that Pausanias describes and how? What words could we use for further commentary of these events? Each one of us: let us come to our own conclusion with reverence and awe about how our ancestors suffered in this place of martyrdom. The acknowledgment of their sacrifice at Callium is an immortal memorial imposing a debt on their descendants, of which we must be worthy bearers and porters of their indescribable sacrifice. And even after the terrible acts, the barbarians stayed in Callium. The plunder and extermination of thousands of martyred residents, the fire and the general destruction of the homes, the public buildings, and the holy shrines of Callium, was not an easy job.[124]

Callium as the capital city was a big city and its destruction was radical and total. Nothing remained standing. Everything was burned. In this general destruction of the buildings were the broken bodies of the old people, the women, and the children who found no mercy from the beastly Galatians. It was a real, complete holocaust that left nothing standing and no one survived in the city. From the most sick and crippled old man, to the youngest small child, to the unborn baby, all were put to death with the most horrible and unbelievable torments that the evil minds of the barbarians imposed upon the people.

Of the most inhumane and indescribable sufferings, however, the women bore the worst sufferings. Many women escaped to the mountains and arrived at Kokkalia, and they fought hard to avoid capture by the Galatians. Those who were captured were killed or abused in the most humiliating way. Pausanias vividly describes the atrocities in the evil way that the Galatians treated the women: "Women and adult maidens, if they had any spirit at all in them, anticipated their end when the city was captured. Those who survived suffered under imperious violence every form of outrage at the hands of men equally void of pity or of love. Every woman who chanced to find a Gallic sword committed suicide. The others were soon to die of hunger and want of sleep, the incontinent barbarians outraging them by turns, and sating their lust even on the dying and the dead."[125]

Callium was totally destroyed and the civilian population was killed. No one survived to tell the story. The Aetolian soldiers, when they returned home to Callium, found no women, children, or old men.

In revenge, the Aetolians subsequently caused the Galatians' total destruction as will be described later in this chapter. As Pausanias says, "...after their arrival at the Spercheios, during the rest of the retreat the Thessalians and Malians kept lying in wait for them, and so took their fill of slaughter that not a Gaul returned home in safety." [Pausanias, *Description of Greece*, The Loeb Classical Library (Harvard University Press, Cambridge, MA, 1979), Trans. W.H.S. Jones, IV, Books VIII (22) – X, p. 507.]

After the Galatians were repelled from Aetolia, Callium began, little by little, to rebuild from its pieces to once again become the glorious capital of Evrytania and to continue in a creative way its historical journey through the Roman and Byzantine ages until its final end by the Turks. This sacrifice became the glory of all of Callium and of all the Aetolians. "The Aetolon, of whom the influence of the Oracle of Delphi was completely uncontested...and during many centuries praises triumphant tone in the shrine of Apollo in order to remind every so often the repulse of the barbarians."[126]

From the Same Path

"The barbarians, having pillaged houses and sanctuaries, and having burned Callium, were returning by the same way..." [Pausanias, X, 22, 6.]

With just a few words but with great clarity, Pausanias describes the tragic aftermath of the catastrophe of Callium, the plunder of the homes and holy centers in Callium, its arson and then the return of the Galatians to Thermopylae from the same way. The barbarian Galatians completely fulfilled their destructive duty at Callium. Now victorious, with their diabolical satisfaction of the calamity they caused to the Callians, and loaded with the treasures stolen from Callium, the Galatians commenced their return to Thermopylae, taking the same path that they came through.

Who would dare to confront or stop the barbarian Galatians? They wanted to hurry to return to Thermopylae to unite with the other Galatian forces and to continue to plunder the rest of Greece. Who would stop them? The women of Aetolia!

Yes, the lion-hearted Aetolian women. The Aetolian women became the vanguard of Callium. For the first time in the history of Greece, and even in the history of the world, we see how these women stood courageously, face to face, to fight the 42,500 Galatian troops, and they crushed them.

And the women who managed to escape from the entrapment and grip of the Galatians in Callium activated the other Aetolian women and elderly men from other nearby cities who had survived. They gathered them to reach a place that is today called Kokkalia (which name will be explained later) and to block the path of the Galatians. In this moment of disaster that had befallen them, the women made a decision that changed the course of history. This decision was pivotal in allowing for the Greek nation to be established, but also the entire European civilization. And this is because of the decision of the Aetolian women to block the road to the Galatians, and to crush them or to die trying. They were determined to achieve the deliverance of the nation. We need to recognize that this effort was not intended just to punish the Galatians for their crimes. It was a decision more so intended for their own deliverance. The women of Callium sought to preserve not only themselves but their region. If they simply wanted to save themselves, they would have only claimed the surrounding mountains and waited until the barbarian Galatians had left. They would have buried their dead and cried. But no, they did not seek something so little and so cheap for the circumstance they were in. They demanded something much more. Something unbelievably great. They demanded to rescue the whole region and all the Greeks from the Galatians. Because if the Galatians had reached their base in Thermopylae without any impediments, NOTHING thereafter would have stopped the Galatians from destroying the rest of the Greek powers. Since the Aetolian army had left Thermopylae to go to protect their own homeland of Aetolia [Pausanias X, 22, 5], if it were not for the women, the Galatians would have destroyed and desecrated everything in their way, even Athens! However, no, the women would never accept that. For them, that would be a national betrayal. And also a humiliation for the dead heroes. It was necessary that the women block the road and crush the Galatians. They considered this their obligation and this is what they did. The women sought to defend the honor and integrity of Aetolia and all of Greece.

The valor of the women was the ultimate self-sacrifice that manifested their tangible love and embrace of the entire Greek region into one country of their own. This act of superhuman heroism and bravery will remain as the ultimate example of sacrifice in all of humanity.

Such an act of bravery by these women was an offering and at the same time a self-sacrifice that went beyond the boundaries of even the self-sacrifices of the ancient pagan world. This act of bravery resembled more closely the love of Christians, which actualizes itself in the God of love. An act springs forth and as such it is completed.

The first task of the women was to send young, fast runners to go as soon as possible to Thermopylae to inform the Aetolian army of the calamity that had befallen them, so that the Aetolian army could help the women quickly [Pausanias X, 22, 5]. And then, the bodies of the dead women, piled high and lined up the length of the road to Kokkalia, formed an unsurpassable, impenetrable wall against the Galatians.

Strategic Position

Before we proceed with the description of the events that took place in Kokkalia in the fall of 279 BC, and the consequences of these events, it is necessary to discuss briefly and to recognize, as much as we possibly can today, the location of the revered place of Kokkalia. And also to discuss briefly the strategic role the location of Kokkalia played in the centuries before Christ.

Kokkalia was a large, strategic location that connected western Greece with the rest of the Greek world throughout the centuries. We must note that the road today that connects western Greece and the rest of Greece, including present-day Karpenisi, did not exist in ancient times. These roads were constructed after the thirteenth century AD.[127] Therefore the only road in ancient times that connected eastern and western Greece was through Thessaly, south of the lake up to the Spercheios Valley in Kokkalia, which was the boundary of Aetolia. From that point, there were three roads:
- On the right was the first road that connected Evrytania and Doris. This road was a very difficult passage, and most of the time impassible.

- The second road, in the Spercheios Valley, connected western Greece with the inhabitants of the entire valley up to Heraclea.
- Finally, the third road was by Kokkalia to the north, on the eastern side of the ridge toward Thessaly passing through the city of Xeniada. This road was the most passable and easiest to travel, by both small and large teams, because the soft soil of the slopes made it easy to pass through the Spercheios Valley and to enter Thessaly.[128] This road easily connected Aetolia with Thessaly for trading and cultural exchanges, but also for military passage. For that reason, the Aetolians used it as a customs station to examine those entering and exiting Aetolia and Thessaly. That is why the Aetolians also constructed a tower[129] and outposts. This was not only to protect them from surprise barbarian attacks, but also to collect duty taxes from traders, farmers, and construction merchants. It is well-known that Aetolia had expanded commerce with Thessaly and Magnesia, even from prehistoric times. This commerce was developed a great deal by the Aetolian Commonwealth, in the fifth to second centuries BC. For this reason, all the import and export commerce of Aetolia needed to pass through Kokkalia and the customs patrol stationed there.

No Ambivalence

Kokkalia, therefore, was a key position for entering and exiting Aetolia. After the destruction of Callium, the Galatians had to follow the same road to return to Thermopylae where the main troops were. It is preposterous that, due to the incorrect assertion by one historian, Soteriades, all Greek historical writers without exception[130] place Callium at Doris (Velouchovo), and not near Kokkalia. How they cannot understand that the smashing of the Galatians happened at Kokkalia by the Aetolians is beyond the comprehension of this author. Fortunately, there are writers who referred to the possibility of Kokkalia as the location where the Aetolians smashed the Galatians. Some of them are the following:

- N.G. Polites. "In the Phtiotida, and the city of Karpenissi, Evrytania: "Laspi, Klapsi, villages of Karpenissi. Klapsi comes from weeping. In this historical event which is referred to according to tradition, is possible that when the invaders Galatians (279 BC) in the massacre of the Callians (inhabitants), swiftly inhabited this area."[131]
- "Made reference to the Evrytanian and Aetolian defense against the Galatians, led by Brennus, in 279 BC in Kokkalia, Krikellou—Laspis, Evrytania, where the Galatians suffered tremendous losses."[132]
- P.I. Vasileiou. "However the aim of Bren-

nus did not succeed, because his hordes of soldiers, after possibly destroying old Klapsi, suffered a great loss in the mountainous place of Kokkalia, between the villages of Agios Nikolaos (previously named Laspi) and Krikello."[133]

- K.A. Romaios (Academician). "The field of battle (or punishment of the Galatians) having Kokkalia, not far from Karpenission…"[134]
- G. Soteriades. "I considered this path was indisputable. Here, in this place, the Galatians left indisputable signs of destruction and according to Pausanias these people suffered greatly. Here we have the field of battle where this destruction occurred."[135]

It is certain therefore, and without ambivalence, that this place is KOKKALIA, acknowledging the dreadful, days long battle of the Aetolians against the cannibalistic Galatians in 279 BC. The fact that everyone accepts that the Galatians suffered great losses at Kokkalia is enough to verify that this place of Callium was in Evrytania. This is enough to support the historical truth that this event took place there.

Research In Loco

While we accept this, it was important to conduct research *in loco*, or "research on the spot." From preliminary visits, we knew that Kokkalia was sown all over with bones on the ground—these were the remains of the murderous battle.

This led us to spend more time in the area, for unofficial visits, to research and to study the exact spot and to consider all aspects of the various opinions. And indeed, from these visits, we observed many important artifacts, which included smashed terracotta roof tiles of various use of the third to fourth century BC. We photographed large boulders that were the remains of a large ancient building. It was a castle, in ruins. And a lot of bones. Countless of thousands of smashed bones, spread in a vast area. This serves as an honest but painful witness to the old and forgotten history of our forefathers and foremothers!

From those informal visits many lectures were held and many articles were published in periodicals and newspapers, so that the events of ancient times in Evrytania may become more generally known to all, so that we may uncover more details, and to determine why the location of Kokkalia was important.

From these lectures and with the publication of this author's book, *Kallion Evrytanias*, there was some movement by the governmental Archeological Office (*Yperesia*) to allow an official visit to the area and to conduct research *in loco*. We were happy to see this movement by the government, and we considered it a first step toward the great archaeological goal to bring to the surface all the buried old glorious history of Evrytania and to restore our historical truth.

This official visit took place on 30 May 1984. The visit included first Kokkalia and then Klapsi, so that the archaeologists could see and examine *in loco* these two important archaeological areas, since both of these places are important.

The organizer and leader responsible for this visit and the mission was Petros Themelis, who at the time was a professor of classical archeology and presiding head (*Proistamenos*) of the Board (*Ephoria*) of Anthropology and Researchers of Caves at the University of Rethymno (Crete). (Here we would like to remind everyone that Mr. Themelis had conducted the excavation of Velouchovo (*Kallion*) in 1977-1979, and that reference was made to Mr. Themelis in Dem. Fallis's book, *Kallion Evrytanias*, p. 81 and p. 197). Also participating in the mission were six others: Theodoros Pitsios, anthropology researcher at the Anthropological Museum of the University of Athens; Voula Rozakis, the presiding head of the Board (*Ephoria*) of Lamia; and Kostas Zahos, a researcher of paleoanthropology and caves; Evangelos Kambouroglou, a geologist and commissioner of paleoanthropology of the Board of Paleoanthropology; Roula Kambouroglou, an architect of the Board of Paleoanthropology; and Theodoros Hatzetheodorou, a surveyor of the Board of Paleoanthropology. Demetrios Fallis, author of *Kallion Evrytanias* and a native of Evrytania, guided the group of experts to the specific archaeological areas with his knowledge of the area.

When we reached Kokkalia, we bent down into the sweet-smelling wildflowers and the water lilies, to see the crushed bones. There were thousands of bones, bleached by the rain, the ice, and the thousands of years, mixed with the soil and the rocks, covered with the love of the sweet-smelling spring wildflowers! It was a silenced, lifeless, locked world; a world which comes from the depth of the centuries until today, to tell us, in its own way, about a tremendous and unrepeatable sacrifice.

Each one of us took in our hands a few pieces of the crushed bones and examined them with curiosity. Each of us brought the pieces close to our eyes to see and to examine them closely.

"There are human bones and animal bones. And there are signs of burning."[136]

All these experts, each one with their own specialty, tried to interpret how and when the dreadful events of Kokkalia took place. They examined even the broken roof tiles, the foundation of the shaved stones, and they walked and examined the entire area. Later we took pictures and we took the road for Karpenisi–Klapsi. At Klapsi, we walked for a long time and examined the ancient areas, the remains of ancient Callium. We admired the design and the embroidery in the floor of the nave of the church of Agios Leonides.

This mission of the seven archaeologists to Kokkalia and to Klapsi, in Evrytania, reached its end with the final conclusion that these two places were very important locations in ancient times. In its report the experts emphasized that "excavations must be done to confirm the history of this place." It is the hope of this author that this will become a reality at some point soon.

How Kokkalia Was Named Before

Based on this, we know that present-day Kokkalia held a strategic location, "the key," in ancient times, for all those who would pass to and from western Greece. It was the natural boundary that separated Aetolia from Doris, and the Spercheios Valley (which was inhabited by the Ainianes), north of which was Thessaly. Finally, we recognize that at Kokkalia the Galatians "suffered great defeat and major loss" at the hands of the Aetolians in 279 BC. The Battle at Kokkalia signified the beginning of the end of the most dangerous invasion by the Galatians that would have wiped out the entire Greek nation.

It is imperative that at this point we stop and examine—to the best of our ability—another side of the history of Kokkalia, which is completely unexcavated and unknown.

We are certain that this location was named Kokkalia based on the plethora of bones dispersed in this large area. It was named this way, we believe, due to the thousands of Aetolian casualties (although we do not know how many Aetolian casualties there were, especially women, who fell in this days-long, savage battle with the Galatians), whose bodies were left to rot in the mountains of Kokkalia, food for the wild mountain beasts, with only the bones remaining.

We are also certain that this place was not named Kokkalia in the last centuries before Christ, or in the first centuries of the Byzantine period. The name "Kokkalia" must have started to be used in the Middle Ages (500 to 1500 AD) during Byzantine or Ottoman times. We believe this is because in the last centuries before Christ, and even to the period of the Middle Ages, "bones" were not called *"kokkala"* like they are today, but *"osta."* Despite all our efforts to verify this in some ancient text or lexicon that the name was the *"osta"* or *"kokkala,"* we were not able to do this. In ancient times, the word *"kokkalo"* was used to describe the core of the pine cone, or the shell of a type of snail on land. Thus, we must hypothesize that it was around the Middle Ages when the word *"osta"* and *"kokkala"* began to be used, especially around 1100–1200 AD, and then, whatever the old name was, it stopped being used.

What was this area named previously, before it was named Kokkalia?

In this author's opinion, this is a very serious question that needs to be answered for the fulfillment of the history of Evrytania. There is so much more to excavate and research. In our research, beyond the problematic questions we raised, we hope we provide some reference points to help other researchers find the historical truth.

Kallidromo

We think that we are not far from the historical truth, if inferentially, we can conclude that this location, which today is known as Kokkalia, was known in ancient times and until the Middle Ages as Kallidromo. However, do not mistake the Kallidromo of ancient times, which we believe was in present-day Evrytania, with the mountain named Kallidromo today. Mount Kallidromo today (formerly called "Saromata") is in the prefecture of Phtiotida, in the area southwest of Thermopylae, east of Mount Oita, which ends abruptly on the Maliako Kolpos (Malian Gulf). We believe the Kallidromo of ancient times was in present-day Kokkalia and was named Kallidromo, which means "good road," because it was a well-established passage in the mountains connecting eastern and western Greece, by way of the southern Thessaly. However present-day Mount Kallidromo does not have an easy passage, and for this reason there is no etymological justification for the name Kallidromo (good road). In addition to the fact that there is no etymological connection for this name for the present-day Mount Kallidromo, we have not been able to find any modern writers who rely on ancient writers to place Kallidromo clearly east of Mount Oita. In fact, many modern writers who write about Kallidromo for various reasons, place Kallidromo west of Mount Oita, in Oxya: "*Kallidromo, (the)*. A mountain, west of Mount Oetis, toward Dysmas."[137]

We do not have space in this book to list all the sources that we have, nor the space for all the analysis and information that supports our conclusion that Kallidromo of ancient times was west of Oites, and not east of Thermopylae. It is imperative therefore that:

- To make reference to a primary, verified source, that: "From 1833-1840, the present-day Province of Evrytania was renamed "Kallidromis" ((B.D. 3) 15 April 1833), and Karpenisi was renamed "Kallidromi," and later it was renamed Oechalia, so that the area could be related to the ancient capital: "Evrytos's City."[138] [*Translator's Note: Later, it was renamed Karpenisi, the current name.*]

The renaming of Karpenisi to Kallidromi took place in 1833 and remained such until 1845. Later the province was named Evrytania, and Karpenisi became the capital city of Evrytania. The Demos of Kallidromo, the area south to southwest of Oxyas (Kokkalia) with a population of 5,472 residents (registered in 1848), included the following villages: Ampliane, Doliana, Domnista, Karya, Kontiva, Marino, Roska, Selitsa, Selos, Stabloi, Ternos, Tsikleista, and Psiana, with the capital of the city of Krikella

(1,312 registered residents in 1856).[139]

We consider the above information to be very important because we see by the actions of our nineteenth century predecessors their desire to connect with their ancient history, that of the ancient Evrytanians (and not simply an irrational worship of the ancients (*archaiolatreias*)).[140] Moreover, these predecessors were closer historically to the events of the Turkish occupation (*Tourkokratias*), and the renaming of places, such as the example of Kallidromo to Kokkalia. It is for this reason perhaps that during this period of the Turkish domination (17th -18th centuries), they renamed this region, possibly Kallidromo, instead of Kokkalia. And this is the conclusion of historic text from the time:

- "During the period of Litzas and Agraphon there was a mountain great and high, which in old Greece was named Orthrys, because it was the mount that you would see at the first of the morning, that is, you would see the coming of the day and the sun first (*protitera*) at this place, more so than all the other mountains of Greece: Lokron, Aetolias, Akarnanon, and Agraphon; now it is called Delouchi, or Velouchi (from the rays of the sun closest to the highest mountain), and along the eastern propodais, is the good-spirited Greece, and on the western side lies the small town of Karpenisi, the home-

land of the new martyr Saint Nicholas, and the seat of Litzas and Agraphon, and the place where the mountain of Mesymvrias meets the Kallidromion and the boundary of Thermopylae of Greece, and the boundless beginnings of Boeotia and Euripou."[141]
- Parallel to the above witnesses is the position of the academician, K.A. Romaios, who notes the following: "The boundless mountain of Oxya, which possibly was named after the ancient Kallidromo."[142]
- Finally: "It is known, and this is certain, that before the horrific event involving the Galatians, it was not named Kokkalia, but some other name, which we do not recognize today. The most possible name was Kallidromo."[143]

They Were Full of Wrath Against the Galatians

Let us repeat and close this small historical study with a description of the most shocking battle that ever happened. It was the battle between the fierce Aetolian women and the 40,800 cannibalistic soldiers of Brennus (leader of the Galatians). The humiliations, the debasements, and the slow torturous deaths that the women of Callium suffered at the hands of the terrible Galatian monsters enraged these fierce surviving women, like lionesses, and made them manic to get revenge.

Kokkalia

As we stated earlier, the Aetolian women sent their fastest young runners to go as fast as they could to Thermopylae, to announce the calamity that had befallen them, so the runners could return quickly to Aetolia. The surviving women of Callium, along with the elderly men and the women of the surrounding villages, blocked the path to Kokkalia, as it was the most strategic position to block the Galatians. That was the decision of the Callium women: to smash the Galatians. The Greeks who fought at Thermopylae had two alternatives, "either conquer or perish" [Pausanias X, 19, 12; Pausanias, *Description of Greece*, The Loeb Classical Library (Harvard University Press, Cambridge, MA, 1979), Trans. W.H.S. Jones, IV, Books VIII (22) – X, p. 479], but the Aetolian women at Kokkalia had only one choice:

To be victorious!

And they were victorious!

They did indeed smash and literally disperse the Galatians and save the entire Greek nation from calamity and vanquishment. Pausanias writes: "From all the cities at home were mobilized the men of military ages; and even those too old for service, their fighting spirit roused by the crisis, were in the ranks, and their very women gladly served with them, being even more enraged against the Galatians than were the men."[144]

Day and night the warfare by the women

against the Galatians continued, without stopping and no break, without food or self-care. The only concern was not to have the barbarians escape. That is why, "They stood lined up along the whole road" [Pausanias X, 22, 6], with axes, with bats, with spears, with knives, rocks, and whatever else they could find, to hold and fight the Galatians. Chest-to-chest, the war continued, and the truly-wounded lionesses blocked the passage of Kallidromos. The entire hill was a mound of human and horse bodies.

When the Aetolian army reached Callium from Thermopylae, the Galatians had no hope of reorganization or victory. Out of the 40,800 initial troops, fewer than half survived. [Pausanias X, 22, 7; Pausanias, *Description of Greece*, The Loeb Classical Library (Harvard University Press, Cambridge, MA, 1979), Trans. W.H.S. Jones, IV, Books VIII (22) – X, p. 495.] There were more than 22,000 Galatian casualties, severely punished for their unheard-of cannibalism in Callium. And of those Galatians who survived, escaping at night through the slopes and ravines of Aetolia, they had no better luck when they arrived in Thermopylae. Perhaps it would have been preferable for them to die in Aetolia. Because being mentally and physically rundown, the Galatians had ended up, from their debacle, together with their embarrassment, preferring to be killed. They carried this embarrassment with them, and fell into disfavor with Brennus, and the common contempt of the other soldiers.

Brennus had heard about this calamity and did not expect their return at all. Embarrassed and resentful, Brennus needed to act quickly to bring results in another strategic way, in order to win the war. After that, he took 40,000 soldiers, guided by the two tribes, Ainianies and the Iraklotes, to go after the Aetolians. Brennus felt the same humiliation that the Persian leader Idarnes had felt. [Pausanias X, 22, 8.] Brennus did finally reach Delphi. But it was too late, because one defeat was to succeed another. And the calamities were coming one after another. Divine and human powers were chasing Brennus, and beat him day and night, until in the end, Brennus was wounded, and then killed himself from his embarrassment. Nobody from the Galatians survived to return to their land.

Monument to the Immortal Glory of the Aetolians

Our age is considered the age of reorganization of our national strength, which is needed to survive creatively as a race and as a nation and in the future to do something creative. It is self-evident that the cornerstone of this reorganization is our national self-knowledge. However, we cannot say today that we have complete national self-knowledge and clear historical identity since part of the Greek nation—Evrytania—played a significant role from ancient times in our historical development, yet it still remains unwritten history and unnecessarily untouched. A characteristic example is Kokkalia, the fiercest historical place of our country, which remains until today the most unknown and most neglected place. It is like an untended vineyard that was ruined.

And yet without the "great war and the massacre"[145] that took place there in 279 BC, it is certain that the Greeks would not have been in existence as a nation.

The wars with the Persians in Marathon, in Salamina, in Plataies, in Thermopylae, and in Mykale, and the general revolt of the Greeks in 1821, which were adopted in our historical courses and which make up the basis of our national pride, led to our ethnic independence and freedom. And it is without a doubt a tremendous contribution to our long course of our history. For that reason, these wars deserve their bright place in history.

However, absent from all this history is the brightest of the thrones: Kokkalia, which was the greatest war and massacre. This was not only for our national independence and freedom, but for our existence as human beings.

An observation of Pausanias is that the Greeks "saw that the impending struggle would not take place for freedom, as it had at the Medika, nor would it have been saved even though they had been offered earth and water"[146] (and as we had analyzed earlier in this book). The historian Pausanias was not exaggerating the massacre at Callium to impress readers. The massacre that took place at Callium at the hands of the Galatians was a tangible reality that was experienced by the Macedonians, the Thracians, the Paiones, the Thessalians, and the cities of Xyniada and Callium, all of which disappeared! [Pausanias, X, 19, 12.]

This war in Kokkalia, therefore, brings us to the conclusion that the apex of the dramatic struggle of our forebears occurred so that we can maintain our existence first as human beings, and then as a free people and a free nation!

And this great sacrifice and the unrepeatable offering of the Aetolians to all the Greeks, everyone acknowledged at that time.

I.G. Papastavrou writes: "Greece was saved from the great danger, and because of this, the great medal (*athlos*) belongs exclusively to the Aetolians, whose influence was the Oracle of Delphi, it was more so undisputed, as is evident from the inscription (SYLL. 534) that memorializes the Aetolians: 'Curating the shrine and the elders.'"

Besides the statues of the generals in the shrine placed in the Delphi monument of Nike, that which represents the heroic Aetolian form is an armed woman, who is seated on a pile of Galatian shields...For many centuries the triumphal hymns echoed in the shrine of Apollo to remind us that every so often of the repelling of the barbarians.[147]

Now is the time to bow again with respect

and awe to the great sacrifice of our forebears and to acknowledge their contribution. Thus, a monument must be set up at Kokkalia (ancient Kallidromo) as a first acknowledgment to give the due respect and tribute and gratitude to the Evrytanian national heroes—men and women—who fell in Kokkalia and Callium so that Greece would be saved.

We assert that this historical monument should be at least equal to other historical monuments of our nation, and even become the brightest and most resplendent. It should be a lighthouse that will illumine all future generations—the bearers of such a glory—so that they will not lose the way of the contribution and sacrifice. A monument in this sacred place, an immortal monument, to the immortal heroes and forebears, and the unrepeatable contribution to our nation, should include the following epitaph:

279 BC
Here, the Evrytanian Champions
Crushed the Galatians as a nation!

ENDNOTES

[1] The history of the Koryskades is very ancient. This is not only because of the findings but from its name, Koryskades, which etymologically comes from the verb *"koryso,"* meaning "I am armed with a helmet," in *perikephalaia* (ancient warrior). The most likely is that in the place both in the mythological and pre-mythical periods there were *perikephalaia*, Koryskadiote K.A. Sarre, *Chroniko Koryskadon*, Athens, 1986, pp. 4-6.

[2] See *Ephimerides, Oi Kastaneotes (Newspaper, The Kastaneotes)*, f. 35 (December, 1986), and *Torniotika Minimata (Torniotika Messages)*, f. 24 (December, 1986).

[3] This tomb is from the Geometric era, and in addition to the human bones which were found there, some copper jewelry was also found, two hairbands, four copper rings, and a sheet of copper metal.

[4] Newspaper, *To Xekinima*, Ekpol. Syll. Palaiokatounas, f. 5, (May, 1986).

[5] Theod. K. Karatzas, *ELLIN, ELLINES, ELLAS*, (Athens, 1971), p. 15.

[6] Athan. Iatrides, *Archaiologike Efemerida (Archaeological Newspaper)*, (Athens, 1838), p. 90. "On Saturday, August 29, 1987, with Mr. John Vrachas we visited the place of Agia Paraskevi Psianon. Following a long walk in the forest and in the rocky area we reached the fortress. We spent a great deal of time

carefully examining the ruins. We admired the fortress with awe. Sufficient parts of the walls, in spite of the thousands of years since its construction, remained intact. The walls consisted of large stones, and the stones were placed with great technique and care in the construction of the fortress from the time of the Pelasgian Age. In this area two tombs were found constructed of stones. It is certain that other tombs exist in this area. We took many pictures. There needs to be an excavation to uncover important objects of the ancient people and civilization. On the road back we encountered a strong downpour and by the time we got back to the church of Agia Paraskevi we were soaked."

[7] Theod. A. Havellas, *Historia ton Aetolon (History of the Aetolians)*, (Athens, 1883), p. 39.

[8] Theod. A. Havellas, *Historia ton Aetolon (History of the Aetolians)*, (Athens, 1883), p. 36.

[9] Sophocles, *Trachinies (The Women of Trachinies)*, Trans. A. Kampane, p. 19 [Also English Trans. Michael Jameson (Chicago: The University of Chicago Press, 1957), p. 85].

[10] Sophocles, *Trachinies (The Women of Trachinies)*, Trans. A. Kampane, pp. 18-19 [Also English Trans. Michael Jameson (Chicago: The University of Chicago Press, 1957), pp. 350-355].

[11] K.A. Romaios, *Megale Enkykl. Drandake (Great Encycl. Drandake)*, v. 2, p. 897, l. Aetolia, and Theod. A. Havellas, *Historia ton Aetolon (History of the Aetolians)*, (Athens, 1883), p. 74, who writes: "The Aetolian unity as manifested in the Homeric Epics."

[12] Theod. A. Havellas, *Historia ton Aetolon (History of the Aetolians)*, (Athens, 1883), p. 27.

[13] It is significant to note that, according to the *En-*

cyclopedia Papyros (v. 11, p. 45), the entries for "Pelasgoi" and the "Pelasgic language" state: "The Pelasgian language was spoken by the Evrytanians during the historical age. All the information we have from ancient authors agrees that the Pelasgians occupied all of Greece. They were seafarers in most of the Mediterranean shores and also inhabited Crete and Phoenicia. The Greeks came from the Pelasgians, the only difference was their language."

[14] Thucydides, *Historion* III 94, Papyros Publications, p. 502. [*Translator's Note: The report that Evrytanians might have eaten raw meat, which was viewed negatively by other Greeks, may not have been true. Although Thucydides recognized the Evrytanians, he recorded ambiguous and rumored information about them. He records precise facts, but only after stating that this information is "rumored" (legontai), and does not confirm it is historical fact. (Marcos A. Guiolias, ton Archaiou Evrytania (Athens 1999) (Editions Poria) (1999), pp. 62-63.) This may have resulted from the enemies of the Evrytanians spreading rumors. For example, Demosthenes who attempted to conquer Evrytania and failed as well the Messenians at Nafpaktos spread false pictures of the Evrytanians (Thucydides III, 94-97).*]

[15] Theod. A. Havellas, *Historia ton Aetolon (History of the Aetolians)*, (Athens, 1883), pp. 27 and 69.

[16] Theod. A. Havellas, *Historia ton Aetolon (History of the Aetolians)*, (Athens, 1883), p. 24.

[17] Theod. A. Havellas, *Historia ton Aetolon, (History of the Aetolians)*, (Athens, 1883), p. 23.

[18] Pausanias, X, 22, 6, Papyros Publications, p. 92.

[19] Mich. G. Houliarakes, *Geographike, Dikitike, kai Plethysmiake Exeleixis tes Ellados 1821-1971 (Geography, Governance, and Population of Greece 1821-1971)*,

(Athens, 1974), pp. 3 ff.

[20] *Enkykl. Hydria (Encycl. Hydria)*, v. 25, p. 138, and *Meg. Soviet Enkykl. (Great Soviet Encycl.)*, v. 12, p. 193.

[21] K.D. Stergiopoulos, *E Archaia Aetolia (Ancient Aetolia)*, (Athens, 1939), p. 83.

[22] P.I. Vasileiou, *Episkope Litzas kai Agraphon (Diocese of Litzas and Agraphon)*, (Athens, 1960), p. 26.

[23] Dem. Fallis, *Kallion Evrytanias*, (Athens, 1982), p. 60.

[24] Homer, *Odyssey*, v. 9, 224, Trans. Iak. Polyla, 1932, p. 84.

[25] Ulrich von Wilamowitz-Moellendorff, *Introduction to Homeric Epic* (Greek Edition), Papyros Publications, p. 8.

[26] Ulrich von Wilamowitz-Moellendorff, *Introduction to Homeric Epic* (Greek Edition), Papyros Publications, pp. 3-4.

[27] Ulrich von Wilamowitz-Moellendorff, *Introduction to Homeric Epic* (Greek Edition), Papyros Publications, pp. 3-4.

[28] N.G. Polites, *Laografika Symmeikta (Folkloric Miscellaneous)*, (Athens, 1920), v. 1, p. 7.

[29] *Lexiko Koinonikon Epistemon (Dictionary of Social Sciences)*, v. 6, p. 4901, entry for *Paradoseis (Tradition)*.

[30] Chr. Th. Papadopoulos, *E Domnista tes Evrytanias (Domnista of Evrytania)*, (Athens, 1961), p. 72.

[31] *Enkykl. Ydria (Encycl. Hydria)*, v. 25, p. 141, entry for *Evrytania*.

[32] Theod. A. Havellas, *Istoria ton Aetolon (History of the Aetolians)*, (Athens, 1883), p. 24.

[33] *Enkykl. Lexiko Eletheroudake (Encyclopedic Dictionary Eleutheroudake)*, v. 6, p. 64, entry for *Evrytos*.

[34] E. Tzanetake, *Enkykl. Ydria (Encycl Hydria)*, v. 21, p. 411, entry for *Dryopes*.

[35] *Megale Enkykl. Drandake (Great Encycl. Drandake)*, v. 9, p. 613, entry for *Dores*.

Endnotes

[36] *Enkykl. Lexiko Eleutheroudake (Encycl. Dictionary Eleutheroudake)*, v. 6, p. 64.

[37] *Apollodoros*, 2, 4, 9 and *Meg. Soviet Enkykl. (Great Soviet Encycl.)*, v. 12, p. 194.

[38] Homer, *Odyssey*, v. 9, 224, Trans. Iak. Polyla, 1932, p. 84.

[39] *Apollodoros*, 2, 4, 9 and *Meg. Soviet Encycl. (Great Soviet Encycl.)*, v. 12, p. 194.

[40] Sophocles, *Trachinies*, Trans. A. Kampane, p. 23.

[41] P.I. Vasileiou, *Archaia Evrytania (Ancient Evrytania)*, (Athens, 1961), p. 11, who writes: "We should note that with the name "Evrytos" we reference five kings with the name Oechalia and six ancient states."

[42] I. Pantazide, *Lexikon Omhrikon (Homeric Dictionary)*, (Athens, 1872), p. 461, entry for *Oechalia*.

[43] *Efemerida Evrytania (Newspaper Evrytania)*, (Athens, 1986), pp. 13-16.

[44] Sophocles, *Trachinies*, Trans. A. Kampane, pp. 18–19.

[45] Sophocles, *Trachinies*, Trans. A. Kampane, pp. 18–19.

[46] K.D. Stergiopoulos, *E Archaia Aetolia (Ancient Aetolia)*, (Athens, 1939), pp. 83–84.

[47] *Strabonas*, 10, 1, 10.

[48] P.I. Vasileiou, *E Archaia Evrytania (Ancient Evrytania)*, (Athens, 1961), p. 11, footnote 5.

[49] P.I. Vasileiou, *Episkope Litzas kai Agraphon (Diocese of Litzas and Agraphon)*, (Athens, 1960), p. 96, footnote 131.

[50] *Sta Ftiothika Hronika (At the Ftiothika Chronicles)*, (Lamia, 1985), p. 6, footnote 1, we read a translation by Ioanna K. Kotsile who studied G.A. Perdicaris, Consul General of the United States in Athens (New York 1846), *E Ellada Ton Ellenon*, that this is the name of Karpenisi (at Kallidromo) from 1833 to 1845.

[51] P.I. Vasileiou, *Episkope Litzas kai Agraphon (Diocese of Litzas and Agraphon)*, (Athens, 1960), p. 120, footnote 175.

[52] K.D. Stergiopoulos, *E Archaia Aetolia (Ancient Aetolia)*, (Athens, 1939), p. 83.

[53] P.I. Vasileiou, *Horia tes Eurytanias pou Katastrafekan (Villages of Evrytania which were Destroyed)*, (Athens, 1969), p. 13.

[54] *Archaeologike Efemerida (Archaeological Newspaper)*, (Athens, 1838), p. 89.

[55] Sp. P. Lambros, *Istoria tes Ellados Met' Eikonon (Illustrated History of Greece)*, (Athens, 1888), p. 657. Critical review of these positions of Sp. P. Lambros in *Efemerida Evrytania (Newspaper Evrytania)*, pp. 19, 21, 27, and 28.

[56] *Megale Enkykl. Drandake (Great Encycl. Drandake)*, v. 2, p. 900.

[57] *Enkykl. Ydria (Encycl. Hydria)*, v. 25, p. 141 and K. Mpaltas, *Kastanea Evrytanias*, (Athens, 1966), p. 30.

[58] P.I. Vasileiou, *E Archaia Evrytania (Ancient Evrytania)*, Athens 1961, p. 17, footnote 22.

[59] Theod. Havellas, *Istoria ton Aetolon (History of the Aetolians)*, (Athens, 1883), p. 24.

[60] K.N. Mpaltas, *Kastanea Evrytanias*, (Athens, 1966), p. 30.

[61] Sp. P. Lambros, *Istoria Tes Ellados Met' Eikonon (Illustrated History of Greece)*, (Athens, 1888), p. 657.

[62] Thucydides, v. 94, Papyros Publications, Trans. Phil. Pappas, p. 503.

[63] Herman Bengtson, *Istoria Tes Archaias Ellados (History of Ancient Greece)*, Melissa Publications, (Athens, 1979), p. 352.

[64] *Megale Enkykl. Drandake (Great Encycl. Drandake)*, v. 2, p. 900 and 897, entry for *Aetolia*.

[65] Theod. Havellas, *Istoria ton Aetolon (History of the Aetolians)*, (Athens, 1883), p. 74.

[66] Theod. Havellas, *Istoria ton Aetolon (History of the*

Aetolians), (Athens, 1883), p. 82.

[67] Dem. Fallis, *Kallion Evrytanias*, (Athens, 1982), p. 83.

[68] *Istoria Eikonografemene (History in Pictures)*, Papyros Publications, no. 205, p. 7.

[69] *Epistole 14 Eforeias Proist. kai Klass. Archaioteton Lamias (Letter XIV from the Council on Prehistoric and Classical Antiquities of Lamia)*, which was published in the newspaper *Evrytania*, 6 November 1985.

[70] In the book review published in Alexandria 1984 by University of Athens Professor Dr. Dem. B. Goni, regarding the study of Dem. Fallis, *Kallion Evrytanias*, (Athens, 1982).

[71] G. Soteriades, *E Ton Galaton Epi Ten Aetolian Efodos, to 279 PX kai e Polis Kallion (The Galatian Attack in 279 BC on the Aetolians and the City of Callium)*, (Paris, 1907), p. 305.

[72] G. Soteriades, *E Ton Galaton Epi Ten Aetolian Efodos, to 279 PX kai e Polis Kallion (The Galatian Attack in 279 BC on the Aetolians and the City of Callium)*, (Paris, 1907), p. 311.

[73] G. Soteriades, *E Ton Galaton Epi Ten Aetolian Efodos, to 279 PX kai e Polis Kallion (The Galatian Attack in 279 BC on the Aetolians and the City of Callium)*, (Paris, 1907), p. 315.

[74] G. Soteriades, *E Ton Galaton Epi Ten Aetolian Efodos, to 279 PX kai e Polis Kallion (The Galatian Attack in 279 BC on the Aetolians and the City of Callium)*, (Paris, 1907), pp. 304-305.

[75] Dem. Fallis, *Kallion Evrytanias*, (Athens, 1982), p. 91.

[76] G. Soteriades, *E Ton Galaton Epi Ten Aetolian Efodos, to 279 PX kai e Polis Kallion (The Galatian Attack in 279 BC on the Aetolians and the City of Callium)*, (Paris, 1907), p. 311.

[77] Dem. Fallis, *Kallion Evrytania*, (Athens, 1982), p. 84.

[78] Pausanias, *Phocica*, Papyros Publications, (Athens, 1969), p. 92.
[79] P.I. Vasileiou, *Episkope Litzas kai Agraphon (Diocese Litzas and Agraphon)*, (Athens, 1960), p. 30.
[80] Dem. Fallis, *Kallion Evrytanias*, (Athens, 1982), p. 94.
[81] Ger. Katopodes, *Aetolike Sympoliteia (Aetolian Commonwealth)*, (Athens, 1977), p. 122.
[82] *Epistole 14 Eforeias Proist. kai Klass. Archaioteton Lamias (Letter XIV from the Council on Prehistoric and Classical Antiquities of Lamia)*, which was published in the *Newspaper Evrytania*, 6 November 1985.
[83] P.A. Pantou, *Ta Sfragismata tes Kallipoleos (The Stamps of Kallipolis)*, (Athens, 1985), p. 3.
[84] W. Smith, *Geographic Dictionary*, (London, 1854), v. 1, p. 65.
[85] W. Woodhouse, *Eastern Aetolia*, (Athens, 1897), p. 371.
[86] K.D. Stergiopoulos, *The Ancient Aetolia*, (Athens, 1939), p. 79.
[87] P.I. Vasileiou, *Horia Tes Eurytanias pou Katastrafekan (Villages of Evrytania which were Destroyed)*, (Athens, 1969), p. 13.
[88] Ger. Katopodes, *Aetolike Sympoliteia (The Aetolian Commonwealth)*, (Athens, 1977), p. 119.
[89] Mikel Dufrenne, *Cahiers Int. De Sociologie*, v. 3 (1947).
[90] N.G. Polites, *Paradoseis (Tradition)*, (Athens, 1904), v. 2, p. 641, no. 10.
[91] Dem. Fallis, *Kallion Evrytanias*, (Athens, 1982), p. 35.
[92] Emanuel Chatzedakes, ΠΑΕ 1958, excavation of the Basilica of Klapsi, p. 61.
[93] Many people from Klapsi who out of curiosity and interest followed the excavations observed that many boxes of various types were discovered, but they do not have any knowledge where these objects

are located now. Pan. Moutoyianis, a former director of the police department, published an account in the periodical Village Echoes (16 March 1982, p. 21). He states: "I was spending my vacation in my village and followed the progress of the excavations and saw important objects, including a very old censer." This censer is not anywhere to be found among the discovered objects.

[94] Dem. Fallis, *Kallion Evrytanias*, (Athens, 1982), p. 118 and p. 123.

[95] Thucydides, v. 3, 113, Papyros Publications, p. 528.

[96] *Pausanias*, X, 22, Papyros Publications, Trans. A. Papatheodorou [Pausanias, *Description of Greece*, The Loeb Classical Library (Harvard University Press, Cambridge, MA, 1979), Trans. W.H.S. Jones, IV, Books VIII (22) – X, pp. 491–493].

[97] Mich. Staphylas, periodiko *Thessalike Estia* (periodical *Thessalian Focus*), (Athens, 1983), v. 65, p. 219.

[98] *Enkykl. Papyros Larous (Encycl. Papyros Larous)*, v. 6, p. 975, entry for *Evrytania*.

[99] Thucydides states, v. III, 94, that the Aetolians (Evrytanians) resided in villages without walls, whereas Pausanias refers to the "cities" [and not villages] in his *Phocis*.

[100] *Enkykl. Papyros (Encycl. Papyros)*, v. 8, p. 390, entry for *Keltai*.

[101] *Enkykl. Papyros (Encycl. Papyros)*, v. 4, p. 698, entry for *Galatia*.

[102] *Enkykl. Papyros (Encycl. Papyros)*, v. 8, p. 392, entry for *Keltikos*.

[103] *Enkykl. Papyros (Encycl. Papyros)*, v. 8, p. 392, entry for *Keltai*.

[104] I.G. Papastavrou, *Archaia Istoria (Ancient History)*, (Athens, 1957), v. 2, p. 252.

[105] G. Soteriades, *E Ton Galaton Epi Ten Aetolian Efodos, to 279 PX kai e Polis Kallion (The Galatian Attack on the Aetolians in 279 BC and the City of Callium)*, (Paris, 1907), p. 303.

[106] Pausanias, X, 19-22, Papyros Publications, Trans. A. Papatheodorou.

[107] Pausanias, X,19,12, Papyros Publications, Trans. A. Papatheodorou [Pausanias, *Description of Greece*, The Loeb Classical Library (Harvard University Press, Cambridge, MA, 1979), Trans. W.H.S. Jones, IV, Books VIII (22) – X, p. 479].

[108] I.G. Papastavrou, *Archaia Istoria (Ancient History)*, (Athens, 1957), v. 2, p. 294.

[109] Pausanias, *The Phocis*, X, 22, 1, Papyros Publications, Trans. A. Papatheodorou [Pausanias, *Description of Greece*, The Loeb Classical Library (Harvard University Press, Cambridge, MA, 1979), Trans. W.H.S. Jones, IV, Books VIII (22) – X, p. 491].

[110] Pausanias, *The Phocis*, X, 22, 1, Papyros Publications, Trans. A. Papatheodorou [Pausanias, *Description of Greece*, The Loeb Classical Library (Harvard University Press, Cambridge, MA, 1979), Trans. W.H.S. Jones, IV, Books VIII (22) – X, p. 489].

[111] Pausanias X, 19, 12, Papyros Publications, p.82, "*Evron de ton en to parondi agona syx yper eleutherias genesomenon katha epi tou Medou pote...*" [Pausanias, *Description of Greece*, The Loeb Classical Library (Harvard University Press, Cambridge, MA, 1979), Trans. W.H.S. Jones, IV, Books VIII (22) – X, p. 479].

[112] Pausanias X, 19, 12, Papyros Publications, Trans. A. Papatheodorou [Pausanias, *Description of Greece*, The Loeb Classical Library (Harvard University Press, Cambridge, MA, 1979), Trans. W.H.S. Jones, IV, Books VIII (22) – X, p. 479].

[113] Pausanias X, 19, 3, Papyros Publications, p. 90 [Pausanias, *Description of Greece*, The Loeb Classical Library (Harvard University Press, Cambridge, MA, 1979), Trans. W.H.S. Jones, IV, Books VIII (22) – X, p. 493].

[114] K. Paparregopoulos, *Istoria Ellinikou Ethnous (History of the Greek Nation)*, (Athens, 1860), pp. 377, 378 and Pausanias X, 20, Papyros Publications, p. 82 [Pausanias, *Description of Greece*, The Loeb Classical Library (Harvard University Press, Cambridge, MA, 1979), Trans. W.H.S. Jones, IV, Books VIII (22) – X, p. 479-491].

[115] Pausanias, X, 19, 9-11, Papyros Publications, p. 80 [Pausanias, *Description of Greece*, The Loeb Classical Library (Harvard University Press, Cambridge, MA, 1979), Trans. W.H.S. Jones, IV, Books VIII (22) – X, p. 481].

[116] Pausanias, X. 20, Papyros Publications, p. 82. In I.G. Papastavrou's book, *Archaia Istoria (Ancient History)*, (Athens, 1957), v. 2, p. 293, Papastavrou raises the number to 30,000 men. He writes: *"Ten diokesin to dynameon, aiopoiai synepasoundo eis 30,000 peripou, anelaven o strategos ton Athenaion Kallipos." Nomizoume omos, oti kai me tes 30,000, den allazei o syshetismos tou annisou agna metaxy Ellenon kai Galaton stis Thermopyles.*

[117] Pausanias X, 19, 12, Papyros Publications, Trans. A. Papatheodorou [Pausanias, *Description of Greece*, The Loeb Classical Library (Harvard University Press, Cambridge, MA, 1979), Trans. W.H.S. Jones, IV, Books VIII (22) – X, p. 479].

[118] Pausanias, X, 21, 1, Papyros Publications, p. 86 [Pausanias, *Description of Greece*, The Loeb Classical Library (Harvard University Press, Cambridge, MA, 1979),

Trans. W.H.S. Jones, IV, Books VIII (22) – X, p. 481].

[119] Pausanias, X, 22, 3, Papyros Publications, Trans. A. Papatheodorou [Pausanias, *Description of Greece*, The Loeb Classical Library (Harvard University Press, Cambridge, MA, 1979), Trans. W.H.S. Jones, IV, Books VIII (22) – X, pp. 485-487].

[120] Pausanias, X, 22, 3, Papyros Publications, Trans. A. Papatheodorou [Pausanias, *Description of Greece*, The Loeb Classical Library (Harvard University Press, Cambridge, MA, 1979), Trans. W.H.S. Jones, IV, Books VIII (22) – X, pp. 485-487].

[121] Newspaper, *Thaumakos*, ekd. *Syllogou Thaumakioton*, k. Arist. Petropoulos, p. 27–29.

[122] The Laestrygones were an ancient savage and cannibal people. According to Homer, Odysseus was lashed by the god of the winds, Aeolos, after six terrible misadventures. The Laestrygones would eat the strangers that came to their city Telepylon. When Odysseus arrived there, he anchored in a safe port with all his ships. He sent his companions to the city. The Laestrygones ate one of them, and then under the leadership of their king Antiphates, the Laestrygones rushed to the port with huge rocks and destroyed all the ships, except that ship which belonged to Odysseus, which managed to leave safely. See Dem. Fallis, *Kallion Evrytanias*, (Athens, 1982), p. 191, footnote 141 [Pausanias, *Description of Greece*, The Loeb Classical Library (Harvard University Press, Cambridge, MA, 1979), Trans. W.H.S. Jones, IV, Books VIII (22) – X, p. 495. Also see Homer, Odyssey IX. 166-542].

[123] Pausanias, X, 22, 3, Papyros Publications, Trans. A. Papatheodorou, and Dem. Fallis, *Kallion Evrytanias*, (Athens 1982), p. 183 [Pausanias, *Description*

of Greece, The Loeb Classical Library (Harvard University Press, Cambridge, MA, 1979), Trans. W.H.S. Jones, IV, Books VIII (22) – X, p. 493].

[124] Dem. Fallis, *Kallion Evrytanias*, (Athens, 1982), pp. 183-184.

[125] Pausanias, X, 22, 4, Papyros Publications, Trans. A. Papatheodorou [Pausanias, *Description of Greece*, The Loeb Classical Library (Harvard University Press, Cambridge, MA, 1979), Trans. W.H. S. Jones, IV, Books VIII (22) – X, p. 493].

[126] I.G. Papastavrou, *Archaia Istoria (Ancient History)*, (Athens, 1957), v. 2, p. 294.

[127] P.I. Vasileiou, *Tourist Guide to Evrytania*, Nomarchias Publications, (1971), p. 68. Indeed, the area around Karpenisi, such as the hill of Agios Demetrios and west of the road of the present-day high school in Karpenisi was inhabited in 2,000 to 3,000 BC. The location of present-day Karpenisi was built and inhabited much later, between the 11th and 13th centuries AD.

[128] *Megale Enkykl. Drandake (Great Encycl. Drandake)*, v. 2, p. 897, entry for *Aetolia*.

[129] It is not out of the realm of possibility that the pile of ruins that are at Kokkalia today was a tower from the Mycenaean civilization (1600-1100 BC); we surmise it to have been first built in the pre-mythical age. Because during the period of Evrytos, that area was the key passage (the gateway) toward Aetolia—where Akarnania and Evrytania had its custom patrol.

[130] Dem. Fallis, *Kallion Evrytanias*, (Athens, 1982), pp. 128–129.

[131] N.G. Polites, *Paradoseis (Tradition)*, (Athens, 1904), Part 2, p. 641, footnote 10.

[132] *Enkykl. Papyros Larous (Encycl. Papyros Larous)*, v.

ST, p. 975, entry for *Evrytania*.
[133] P.I. Vasileiou, *Horia tes Eurytanias pou Katastrafekan (Villages of Evrytania which were Destroyed)*, (Athens, 1969), p. 13.
[134] *Megale Enkykl. Drandake (Great Encycl. Drandake)*, v. 2, p. 899.
[135] G. Soteriades, *E Ton Galaton Epi Ten Aetolian Efodos, to 279 PX kai e Polis Kallion*, (Paris, 1907), p. 317. And on p. 310 of the same book: "That by the path (of Kokkalia) was indisputable, here in this place left indisputable signs of their disaster, and according to Pausanias, these people suffered the field of battle in which the catastrophe occurred." "*Entautha (sta Kokkalia) ethrausthi pleon pasa afton antistasis. Sproxthentes eis ta koilomata tis theseos to kokkalion, eno ta perix ypsomata katelampanonto apo Aetolous, adynaton na diaphygosi dia ton pyknon dason, opou opisthen pantos dendrou enhdreuen exthros.*"
[136] This visit of the archaeologists to Kokkalia was reported in the journal, *Horiatikoi Antilaloi*, (1984), v. 26, pp. 69–72.
[137] S. Boutyra and G. Karydou, *Lexiko Istoriko kai Geografiko (Historical and Geographical Dictionary)*, (Constantinople, 1881), entry for *Kallidromo*.
[138] P.I. Vasileiou, *Episkope Litzas kai Agraphon (Diocese Litzas and Agraphon)*, (Athens, 1960), p. 120, footnote 175.
[139] a) Mich. G. Houliarakes, *Geographike, Dikitike, kai Plethysmiake Exeleixis tes Ellados 1821–1971 (Geography, Governance, and Population of Greece 1821-1971)*, (Athens, 1974), v. 1, p. 3 and p. 21; A.B. Kosta Zese, *Agraphiotes kai Karpenisiotes, Agonistes tou 1821 (Agraphiotes and Karpenisiotes, Warriors of 1821)*, Athens 1983, pp. 120-137. b) Kosta Zese, *Agrafiotes kai Karpenesiotes Agonistes tou 1821*, (Athens, 1983), pp. 420-437.

[140] P.I. Vasileiou, *Episkope Litzas kai Agraphon (Diocese Litzas and Agraphon)*, (Athens, 1960), p. 120.
[141] Iera Thiageseis, *Panagia Prousiotissa*, (Athens, 1983), pp. 61-62.
[142] *Megale Enkykl. Drandake (Great Encycl. Drandake)*, v. 2, p. 897, entry for *Aetolia*.
[143] Dem. Fallis, *Kallion Evrytanias*, (Athens, 1982), p. 173.
[144] Pausanias, X, 22, 5, Papyros Publications, p. 92.
[145] N.G. Polites, *Paradoseis (Tradition)*, Part 1, p. 7, no. 10.
[146] Pausanias, X, 19, 12, Papyros Publications, Trans. A. Papatheodorou [Pausanias, *Description of Greece*, The Loeb Classical Library (Harvard University Press, Cambridge, MA, 1979), Trans. W.H.S. Jones, IV, Books VIII (22) – X, p. 479].
[147] I.G. Papastavrou, *Archaia Istoria (Ancient History)*, (Athens, 1957), v. 2, p. 294.

AFTERWORD

Nicholas and Jane Kourtis

Growing up in the USA, our parents instilled in us a love for their homeland of Greece, her history, language, and people. We felt a special connection with Evrytania. Nick's father is from Proussos, where the famous and revered monastery of Panagia Proussiotissa is nestled in a rugged canyon. Jane's father is from Petralona and Hohlia, northeast of Karpenissi. Through the years we have been involved in our local Evrytanian society, and we know many good people who came from this region of Greece or are descendants of them. We appreciate their devotion to the Hellenic ideals and their deep Greek Orthodox faith.

It was not until reading this outstanding book that we fully understood the contributions of the ancient Evrytanians and their far-reaching impact. This book sets out the profound history of the ancient Evrytanians, their first King Evrytos, and the Evrytanian warriors, including the heroic Aetolian women warriors. It describes the fierce determination of this ancient people against barbaric invaders. We read about how the ancient Evrytanians bonded with the rugged and mountainous land, and with each other, to survive. The determination of the ancient Evrytanians has carried through to the present day. We continue to see the dedication of the Evrytanians to their homeland and their faith.

We express our appreciation to Mr. Demetrios Fallis and to Rev. Fr. George Papademetriou (Jane's father) for their devotion to ensure that this important history was not lost. Each of them was equally insistent that this book be translated into English for the diaspora. We thank them profusely for their love of their beloved Evrytania, and for their resolve in seeing this work through to fruition. We thank the publisher, Dean Papademetriou and Somerset Hall Press, for taking on the publication of this invaluable translation.

We encourage all Evrytanians and all enthusiasts of history to own a copy of this book and to read about the astounding story of the ancient Evrytanians!

Attorneys Nicholas and Jane Kourtis reside in Needham, Massachusetts.

PICTURES OF EVRYTANIA

Welcome to Velouchi

Mount Velouchi

On Mount Velouchi, Fr. George Papademetriou (center)
with his sons and grandsons (left to right):
Dean, George, Roman, and Tom

A mountain pass on the road to Proussos

The mountainous terrain of Evrytania

The Monastery of the Panagia in Proussos

Sculpture of Dionysos (second century BC), found in 1935 near present-day Petralona and Hohlia (mentioned on page 30)

Mosaic floor from the church of Agios Leonides,
Klapsi (further described on page 80)

Graphic of the mosaic floor from the church
of Agios Leonides

Mosaic floor from the church of Agios Leonides

Mosaic floor from the church of Agios Leonides

Inscription on the Holy Altar (see page 82)

Icon of Agios Leonides and the Seven Female Disciples

ABOUT THE AUTHOR

Mr. Demetrios Fallis hails from Evrytania, Greece. He was born and raised in Klapsi, Evrytania (which he asserts is ancient Callium). In 1946 he left Klapsi for Karpenisi and then later for Athens, where he was educated at the Eboroke Schole. After various jobs, he opened his own business where he worked until his retirement 1990. Throughout the years Mr. Fallis was a regular member of the Christianikes Enoseos Ergazomenes Neolaias where he wrote numerous articles in the monthly periodical, *Ergatiko Fos*. At the same time Mr. Fallis devoted himself to the study of the history of his hometown, Klapsi, and of Evrytania generally. He conducted in person research from village to village in Evrytania. He wrote numerous articles under a pseudoynym, Brahos, until 1995 at which time he revealed this in a book entitled, *Tes Pistes kai tes Patridas*. Mr. Fallis has written books and lectured widely on the history of Evrytania. In addition to *Evrytania: Ancient History and Legend*, he is the author of *Kallion Evrytanias, Storike Anadrome B.D. Parnassidas*, and *O Agios Leonides the Martyr*.

ABOUT THE TRANSLATOR

Fr. George Papademetriou hails from Evrytania, Greece. His paternal grandfather was Georgios Papademetriou (also called Papadonikos) from Petralona. His maternal grandfather was Konstantinos Katsifas from Hohlia. In 1939, his father, Fr. Constantine Papademetriou, a priest and a teacher, came to America to serve the Greek Orthodox Archdiocese of America in a parish and to teach Greek to children of Greek immigrants. Fr. George came to America several years later, after World War II. After high school he graduated from Holy Cross seminary in Brookline, MA and became a priest. While serving parishes in the U.S., Fr. George received a PhD and other graduate degrees and became the director of the library and professor at Hellenic College/ Holy Cross Greek Orthodox School of Theology for many years. He has published numerous books and articles on world religions, philosophy, hesychasm, and the Greek Orthodox faith and heritage. Now he is retired and emeritus.

Selected Books from Somerset Hall Press

Aivali: A Story of Greeks and Turks in 1922, by Soloup.

Americans and the Experience of Delphi, edited by Paul Lorenz and David Roessel.

Christian Faith and Cultural Heritage: Essays from a Greek Orthodox Perspective, by Demetrios J. Constantelos.

The Church and the Library: Studies in Honor of Rev. Dr. George C. Papademetriou, edited by Dean Papademetriou and Andrew Sopko.

Church and Society: Orthodox Christian Perspectives, Past Experiences, and Modern Challenges; Studies in Honor of Rev. Dr. Demetrios J. Constantelos, edited by George P. Liacopulos.

Dante and Byzantium, by E.M. Karampetsos. An analysis of the Byzantine art and theology on Dante's thought and writings.

Fate and Ambiguity in Oedipus the King, by Stelios Ramfos, translated by Norman Russell. A literary and philosophical reflection on the world-famous play, with a Foreword by renowned actor Olympia Dukakis.

Myth and the Existential Quest, by Vassilis Vitsaxis, translated by Deborah Brown Kazazis and Vassilis Vitsaxis.

Odysseus: A Verse Tragedy, by Nikos Kazantzakis, translated by Kostas Myrsiades.

Orthodox Christian Views of Other Religions: Interfaith Studies, by George C. Papademetriou.

Pomegranate Seeds: An Anthology of Greek-American Poetry, edited by Dean Kostos.

Presbytera: The Life, Mission, and Service of the Priest's Wife, by Athanasia Papademetriou.

Shinjo: Reflections, edited by Anton Pantzikas. A compilation of the writings and ideas of the Japanese Buddhist master Shinjo Ito.

Thought and Faith: Comparative Philosophical and Religious Concepts in Ancient Greece, India, and Christianity, by Vassilis Vitsaxis, translated by Deborah Brown Kazazis and Vassilis Vitsaxis.

Two Traditions, One Space: Orthodox Christians and Muslims in Dialogue, edited by George C. Papademetriou.

The Virgin Mary in Holy Icons and Stories, by Athanasia Papademetriou.

Somerset Hall Press specializes in scholarly and literary books, including history, theology, philosophy, poetry, and Greek studies. For more information about these books, please visit www.somersethallpress.com.

www.ingramcontent.com/pod-product-compliance
Lightning Source LLC
Chambersburg PA
CBHW072014110526
44592CB00012B/1303